Against the Iroquois

AGAINST THE IROQUOIS

The Sullivan Campaign of 1779 in New York State

Fon W. Boardman, Jr.

Henry Z. Walck, Inc.
A Division of
David McKay Company, Inc.
New York

Copyright © 1978 by Fon W. Boardman, Jr.

All rights reserved, including the right to reproduce this book, or parts thereof, in any form, except for the inclusion of brief quotations in a review.

Library of Congress Cataloging in Publication Data

Boardman, Fon Wyman, 1911-
   Against the Iroquois.

  Bibliography: p. 103
  Includes index.
  1. Sullivan's Indian Campaign, 1779. 2. Sullivan, John, 1740-1795. 3. New York (State)—History—Revolution, 1775-1783. I. Title.
E235.B68   973.3'35   77-014918
ISBN 0-8098-0014-4

10 9 8 7 6 5 4 3 2 1

Manufactured in the United States of America

A Note of Thanks

I am happy to acknowledge my debt to the Chemung County Historical Society of Elmira, New York, and to express my thanks to it and its staff. Mr. Richard I. Weiss, acting executive director, and Mrs. Martha Kelsey Squires, history research and librarian, were most helpful in providing me with research material and facilities during a visit to the society's historical center. Mr. Alfred C. Hilbert, historian for the society, kindly gave me a guided tour of the Newtown battlefield, with which he is far more familiar today than General Sullivan was in 1779. One understands very clearly why one wing of the American army was held up when one pauses within a few yards of the same swamp the men struggled through two hundred years ago.

During my stay in Elmira it seemed to me the society demonstrates that with good will and hard work a historical association such as this can preserve the past and illuminate history to today's generation without large sums of money or elaborate structures, fine as they may be. Finally, I was especially pleased to find that the people of the Southern Tier of upstate New York, my own native region, remain friendly, courteous, and helpful to strangers.

July 1977   F. W. B., Jr.

Contents

A Note of Thanks   v

List of Illustrations   ix

"... most barbarously murdered"   1

"... the only savages capable of refined feelings"   19

"... total destruction and devastation"   39

"The troops were much animated"   57

"The land exceeds any that I have ever seen"   69

"... the very graves of their fathers"   87

A Reading List   103

Index   105

Illustrations

Map of the Route of the Sullivan Expedition   54
Map of the Battle of Newtown   64
Portrait of Major General John Sullivan   3
Portrait of Joseph Brant   12

Against the Iroquois

"... most barbarously murdered"

Between five and six o'clock on the morning of June 18, 1779, Major General John Sullivan led an expeditionary force of Continental Army troops out of Easton, in east central Pennsylvania. The force consisted of approximately three thousand officers and men from Massachusetts, New Hampshire, New Jersey, and Pennsylvania regiments, together with artillery, pack horses, and other materials and equipment that accompany such an expedition. General Sullivan had been in Easton since May 7, assembling his army, which also included boats to be used in carrying supplies up the Susquehanna River.

The expedition's first goal was Wyoming, fifty-eight miles northwest of Easton, where the army would make its final preparations and gather the rest of its supplies. Then it would plunge into an almost uncharted area of mountains and forests on a route continuing northwest. The march would take the army into New York State and, if all went according to plan, as far north and west as Fort Niagara at the mouth of the Niagara River on Lake Ontario. The objective of General Sullivan's campaign was to break the power of the Iroquois Indians who, with the aid of British troops and American Loyalists, had been killing settlers and destroying houses and villages in northeastern Pennsylvania and eastern and central New York. The situation, in fact, had reached the point where many people feared that this whole area might have to be abandoned to the British and their Indian allies.

As it turned out, Sullivan's expedition was the only American campaign of the Revolution aimed primarily at Indian enemies and the only major offensive waged by the rebel colonists in 1779.

New York was the only one of the thirteen rebelling colonies in which Indian war strength was an important factor on the British side. Because of New York's location in relation to the other colonies and the geographical pattern of its settlements, this fact put the colonial forces at a disadvantage and greatly worried their leaders, including General George Washington. If control of New York fell to the British, the New England colonies would be cut off from the others to the south, with perhaps fatal consequences to the American Patriots' cause. The distribution of New York's population also favored the British. There were about 200,000 inhabitants in the colony at the start of the Revolution, somewhat less than 10 percent of the total colonial population of about 2,750,000. However, almost all the inhabitants lived on Long Island, in New York City, or along the Hudson River. Comparatively few pioneers had pushed westward along the Mohawk Valley and into other areas in central New York. Many of these small settlements were isolated, and this was the very area where the strength of the Iroquois Indians and the British Loyalists was greatest.

The Iroquois Indians had a long history of alliance with the British. In the series of wars between Great Britain and France, which began as far back as 1689 and which were worldwide in scope, the Iroquois rendered valuable service to the British in the North American phase of this imperial conflict for colonies. The alliance was cemented in the final struggle, known in North America as the French and Indian War, which was fought between 1756 and 1763 and which resulted in complete victory for the British. The French surrendered Canada, leaving Great Britain supreme in North America and making the Iroquois more than ever the domi-

Major General John Sullivan. From the painting attributed to Richard Morell Stargg. *Courtesy Independence National Historical Park Collection, Philadelphia, Pennsylvania.*

nant Indian group in the entire northeastern part of the continent.

One reason for Britain's success in winning and keeping the powerful and warlike Iroquois on its side was the manner in which the English treated the Indians. They did not make them feel inferior; the Iroquois' advice in matters of strategy and tactics was listened to; and guns, metal tools, cloth, and other products of the white man's civilization were distributed on a generous scale.

One man in particular had a great deal to do with making and strengthening the alliance that was so successful until the events of the American Revolution divided the Iroquois as well as the colonists. He was Sir William Johnson (1715–74), who was born in Ireland and emigrated to America in 1738. He settled in the Mohawk Valley, in the area of present-day Amsterdam, and became a successful trader with the Indians. Johnson had a commanding presence and was an eloquent speaker, but he owed most of his success to his honesty in most of his dealings with the Indians and to his life-style in which he wore Indian dress and entertained them in his home. He became a large landowner and built a mansion known as Johnson Castle.

For his services to the British crown, Johnson was knighted in 1755. That same year he was made superintendent of Iroquois affairs and the next year was named general superintendent of all Indian matters in the territory north of the Ohio River. Johnson was active in the French and Indian War and commanded the force that captured Fort Niagara from the French. His prestige enabled him to negotiate with the Iroquois in 1768 the Treaty of Fort Stanwix (now the city of Rome). In return for extensive and fairly valuable presents, the Indians by this treaty ceded to the British large areas of land in central New York, in Pennsylvania, and in areas farther south that were inhabited by tribes dependent on the Iroquois. The treaty was unfavorable to the Indians. Johnson died suddenly in November 1774 during a council meeting with Indian leaders.

Sir William's successor, as war between the colonies and their mother country was about to break out, was Guy Johnson (c. 1740–88), who was also born in Ireland, was Sir William's nephew, and came to America and married his daughter. Guy served in the French and Indian War and during the Revolution was instrumental in keeping the Iroquois, on the whole, faithful to the British alliance. It was not easy to do this because the Indians were greatly puzzled by what seemed to them to be an unnecessary quarrel between brothers. At the start, many of them were of a mind to keep out of such a quarrel entirely.

For example, when the Iroquois heard of the Boston Tea Party of December 1773, during which rebellious colonists threw tea arriving in Boston harbor overboard so that the tax imposed on it by the British government would not be paid, Guy Johnson tried to explain away the affair as a masterly bit of oversimplification:

> This dispute was solely occasioned by some people, who not withstanding a law of the King and his wise Men, would not let some Tea land, but destroyed it, on which he was angry, and sent some Troops with the General, whom you have long known, to see the Laws executed and bring people to their sences, and as he is proceeding with great wisdom, to shew them their great mistake, I expect it will soon be over.

Guy Johnson was somewhat overoptimistic and soon found himself directing his Indian allies in raids against frontier settlements inhabited by those who took up the Patriots' cause. He made his headquarters at Fort Niagara from 1779 on.

Guy was aided by Sir John Johnson (1742–1830), son of Sir

William, who was born in the Mohawk Valley. At the start of the Revolution he also worked hard to organize the Indians and Loyalists to raid the villages of those who favored the Rebels. The Rebels, for their part, determined to capture John, who was forced to flee to Montreal to escape them. Later he returned to New York and led raids in the Mohawk and Schoharie valleys. John was knighted in 1765, and in 1782 he succeeded his brother-in-law Guy as superintendent of Indian affairs with headquarters in Canada.

The revolutionary cause was in jeopardy in New York from the start of the war. An American campaign to take Quebec, Canada, in 1775, ended in defeat at the end of the year, leaving the colony wide open to attack from the north by the British forces in Canada. In late June 1776 a large British fleet and army arrived in New York harbor and prepared to attack the force General Washington had assembled to defend the city. The Patriots were badly defeated at the Battle of Long Island on August 27 by General Sir William Howe, and within two months, in spite of delaying tactics on Washington's part, the Continental Army had been forced north of the city into central Westchester. The British thus controlled the lower Hudson River Valley and the invasion route northward.

With these circumstances favoring them, the British planned for 1777 a three-pronged attack intended to split New York, and hence the thirteen colonies, in two. The main effort was to be made by General John Burgoyne, marching south from Canada along Lake Champlain and heading for Albany, New York. There if all went well, he would meet up with another British force that was to ascend the Hudson River from New York and a third force sweeping through the Mohawk Valley eastward.

Burgoyne began his southward march in June with a total of about 9,500 troops, including four or five hundred Indians. Most of these were from Canada or from the west, and few if any seem to have been from Iroquois territory in New York. Burgoyne specifically ordered the Indians not to kill and scalp

"... most barbarously murdered" 7

old men, women, children, and wounded Patriot soldiers. The Indians turned out to be more interested in pillaging and looting than in helping the British defeat the Americans, although only one Indian atrocity was reported. Near Fort Edward on July 27, a young woman, Jane McCrea, was captured, and an Indian warrior then killed, scalped, and mutilated her. Burgoyne at first threatened to have the warrior executed, but on being told that if he did all the Indians would desert him, decided to do nothing.

The Americans made the most of the incident, spreading word of it around the area. The result was an increase in volunteers, especially from nearby New England, of men resolved that such a thing would not happen in their home towns. Major General Horatio Gates, who took command of the American army opposing Burgoyne in August, helped publicize the incident. Gates's army was augmented in September by about 150 Iroquois of the Oneida and Tuscarora tribes who had decided to abandon the British. They proved to be loyal and dependable, and one observer noted that they were "Brave men and fought like Bull dogs." Meanwhile, Burgoyne's Indians were proving of little use and before the end of September all but about fifty of them had defected and gone home.

One reason for their defection was the fact that the British campaign was making very slow progress and was bogging down on the difficult march through forests toward Albany. Also, as time went on, the Americans grew in strength and continually harried the British forces as they plodded forward. By mid-October, Burgoyne's advance ground to a halt near Saratoga, New York, and after a final battle he surrendered his entire army on October 17. It was the first major victory of the war for the American forces.

In the end, all three parts of the planned campaign failed. To the south, General Howe was engaged in capturing Philadelphia and General Sir Henry Clinton was left in command in New York. Clinton was slow to carry out his part of the plan and did not seem enthusiastic about it. In the summer he began an advance up the Hudson, which for a while gave the Americans cause for worry. He broke through their defenses and got as far north as Kingston on October 15. He went no farther and shortly thereafter returned to New York so that some of his troops could be sent to assist General Howe in Pennsylvania.

Although the third prong of the campaign failed also, it resulted in one bloody battle with Loyalists pitted against Patriots, demonstrating that the Revolution was a civil war of neighbor against neighbor as well as a revolt against a distant monarchy. The Mohawk Valley campaign was commanded by General Barry St. Leger (1737–89), who had fought in the French and Indian War. His army of about fourteen hundred men included British regular troops, some American Loyalists (or Tories), some Canadians, and between six and eight hundred Iroquois. This formidable force appeared before Fort Stanwix on August 2, 1777, and laid siege to the Patriots' strongest position in the valley. The fort was commanded by twenty-eight-year-old Colonel Peter Gansevoort (1749–1812), a New Yorker who had joined the army in 1775.

To meet the treat to Stanwix, the Patriots organized a force of about eight hundred militiamen, under the command of Brigadier General Nicholas Herkimer (1728–77), to march toward the fort from the east. St. Leger sent a detachment of some four hundred Indians and a number of Tory Rangers to turn back the militia. Herkimer, who had earlier been accused of being too cautious, this time resolved to show his spirit. As a result, on August 6 he led his men into an ambush and a bitter hand-to-hand battle that went on for hours. The Indians and British eventually withdrew, carrying away many prisoners, but unwilling to fight any longer. The Patriots suffered about two hundred casualties and their attackers nearly as many. Herkimer was mortally wounded and his force fell back along the Mohawk in the direction from which it had come.

In spite of the failure of this relief expedition, and even

though food and ammunition ran low, Gansevoort and his garrison of 450 soldiers held out. St. Leger attacked and threatened, but when word reached the area that General Benedict Arnold and a thousand Continentals were on the way to relieve Fort Stanwix, the British besiegers lost heart. Their Indian allies had already had enough of this unprofitable warfare and deserted in a body. St. Leger lifted the siege and retreated to Canada.

While the British plans for 1777 ended in defeat and disaster, the situation in central New York remained much as it had been: Loyalists and Indians pitted against Patriots, with feeling running higher all the time. Further bloodshed could be anticipated for 1778, and the Iroquois would have a large part in it. The first major blow was struck on May 30, 1778, against Cobleskill, only about thirty-five miles west of Albany. As was to be true of other attacks throughout the year, the British force consisted mostly of Loyalists and Iroquois. Few British regulars were available. About three hundred Loyalists and Indians were sufficient to overcome the Cobleskill defenders, burn the town, and plunder the ruins.

In September, a similar force laid waste to farms for ten miles along the Mohawk area of German Flats, near Herkimer. The next month it was the turn of Unadilla, a settlement on the Susquehanna River northeast of Binghamton. Nearly a year later, while General Sullivan was still at Wyoming making his final preparations, the Tories and Indians on July 20, 1779, struck Minisink, far down in southern New York on the Delaware River and therefore no great distance from Wyoming. The settlers who supported the Revolution and who suffered these attacks saw them as the loosing of savagery on civilized people and as bloodthirsty revenge on the part of Loyalists who opposed the Revolution. While the raids included these elements, they were actually carefully planned as a means of weakening the rebel army indirectly. The destruction of farms and crops prevented the Patriots from supplying the Continental Army with food and horses and fodder for the latter. At the same time, as shown by the Sullivan expedition, the attacks forced the Americans to take troops away from direct confrontation with the British army in order to protect this frontier area.

The guiding minds behind these and other raids on Patriot farms and villages were those of two white men and one Mohawk Indian. They led most of the raids in person. John Butler (1728–96) was born in Connecticut and moved to the Mohawk Valley with his father in 1742. He served under Sir William Johnson in the French and Indian War, leading the Iroquois who helped capture Fort Niagara. At that place in May and June 1776, while acting superintendent of Indian affairs, he made an impassioned plea to the Iroquois to hold to their alliance with the British and to take up arms against the Patriots. The Indians refused to "declare war," being still baffled as to why white brother was fighting white brother. Colonel Butler, who was described as "short and fat but active," organized what became in the eyes of the Patriots the most hated military unit of all: Butler's Rangers, made up of American Tories. Butler was with St. Leger at the unsuccessful siege of Fort Stanwix.

Walter Butler (1752?–81) was the son of John Butler and was as fervent a Loyalist as his father. Captured by the Patriots in 1777, he was sentenced to death but was granted a reprieve. He escaped in April 1778 and was an active leader of the Rangers thereafter. Walter was killed in what was probably the last battle of the Revolution fought in New York, in late October 1781. In this affray, which took place ten days after General Cornwallis surrendered at Yorktown, Virginia, Butler was leading a unit of the Rangers when he was shot in the head. An Oneida Indian scalped him and sent the scalp to Albany.

The foremost Iroquois leader on the British side, a man who was as fanatically pro-English as any of the Loyalists, was Joseph Brant (1742–1807). His Indian name was Thayendanegea and he was a war chief of the Mohawks. Taken in as a teenager by Sir William Johnson, Brant was sent to school in Connecticut and was one of the first of his tribe to learn to read and write English. He also became a very devout member of the Anglican Church and translated the *Book of Common Prayer* into the Mohawk language. Brant fought in the French and Indian War and Johnson in return made him a colonel.

Guy Johnson took him to England with him at the time the Revolution was breaking out, so Brant missed the first phases of the war. In London Brant was a social success and was much sought after. The popular artist George Romney painted his portrait. Johnson and Brant returned to America in July 1776, and Brant was soon hard at work trying to keep the Iroquois on England's side. The next year he fought at the battle of Oriskany and thereafter was a leading figure in many raids on Patriot settlements. After the Revolution, the British granted Brant and his followers land in Canada and they settled around what is now Brantford, Ontario.

To the American side, Brant was one of the most bloodthirsty creatures who ever lived, and he was accused of massacres and atrocities that occurred on occasions when he was not present. He did follow Indian practices of the time, which included killing prisoners taken in battle and wounded prisoners who could not keep up with the pace of the march. The torture of prisoners captured by the Indians was accepted among them, and every warrior knew it quite likely would happen to him if he were taken prisoner, but there is no record of Brant ever having personally participated in such torture. He never harmed women or children and usually treated males who were not combatants in a humane manner.

These three men were responsible for the two most savage raids of 1778, raids that resulted in heavy casualties among men, women, and children. The raids also resulted in cries for revenge and for assistance from the Continental Army and so were partly responsible for the Sullivan expedition. One of these two attacks on Patriot settlements took place in the

Joseph Brant by Gilbert Stuart, 1786. *New York State Historical Association, Cooperstown.*

Wyoming Valley of northeastern Pennsylvania, the other at the village of Cherry Valley in east central New York.

The Wyoming Valley is about twenty miles long and three to four miles wide, lying along the Susquehanna River. Wilkes-Barre is the chief city of the area. The Indian name for the valley, which was shortened into Wyoming, means "big flats" or "large plains." (The far western state of Wyoming thus has no native claim to the name. When that area was organized as a territory in 1868, a congressman from Ohio suggested calling it Wyoming. Opponents thought an eastern name not appropriate but they couldn't agree on any other; there was considerable interest in Indian names at the time; and the meaning of the word was fitting for the western plains. Thus the word moved west.)

A group of colonists purchased a large area of land in the Wyoming Valley from the Indians in 1754, and the first permanent settlement was made in 1769. Later the Indians felt they had been cheated in the deal and they were probably right. By 1778 the valley was a thriving farming area, with several forts, including the main strong point, Forty Fort. Then, on June 30, a force of Rangers and Indians appeared on the scene. They numbered 110 Rangers and about 465 Indians, mostly Senecas, but including some from other Iroquois tribes. The force was commanded by John Butler and among the Indian leaders was Cornplanter (c.1740–1836). Cornplanter had a white father and became a leading chief of the Senecas. He had great influence over his tribe and did much to keep it on the British side during the war. Later he advocated friendship with the whites and he was given a grant of land on the Allegheny River in western New York where he lived to be nearly one hundred.

Also among the Indian warriors were Handsome Lake (1735?–1815) and Red Jacket (c.1758–1830). Handsome Lake was a half-brother of Cornplanter and in later life became a religious leader, preaching to the Indians a religion similar in content to Christian ethics. He also advocated giving up the traditional Indian way of life and adopting a settled agricultural existence. Red Jacket, who became a prominent Seneca chief, was only twenty years old at Wyoming, but he was already beginning to acquire among his fellow warriors a reputation for cowardice in battle that he never overcame. His name was given him because of a red British uniform coat he wore during the Revolution. Later he strongly opposed Handsome Lake's attempt to change the religion and way of life of the Indians.

The American forces in the Wyoming Valley were under the command of Colonel Zebulon Butler (1731–95), born in Massachusetts and a veteran of the French and Indian War. He had been one of the first settlers in the area, leading a group of pioneers from Connecticut. His force consisted of about four hundred men, of whom sixty were regulars and the rest militia. Instead of waiting to be besieged, Colonel Butler led his troops out of Forty Fort on July 3 to find the invaders and to try to drive them away. Major John Butler ordered his Rangers and Indians to act as though they were retreating, then posted them so that if the Americas continued to advance they would march into an ambush, with Rangers on one side and Indian warriors on the other. The invaders held their fire even after three volleys from the Americans, then fell on them, outflanked them, and drove them back. The retreat turned into a rout and more than three hundred of the Americans were killed or captured. Colonel Butler fled the area while the few remaining troops reached Forty Fort in safety. The invaders counted 227 scalps taken. Their own losses were very light, John Butler claiming that only one Indian and two Rangers were killed and eight Iroquois wounded.

The next day the fort surrendered and the Patriots were promised they would not be molested. John Butler, however, was unable to control the Indians, who began looting houses and barns. Butler himself estimated that one thousand homes were burned. All the mills were destroyed and a thousand head of livestock driven off.

While the Indians undoubtedly killed some prisoners, probably by making them run the gauntlet, and while there was much suffering among the inhabitants of the area, the stories that soon circulated about a horrible "massacre" were not true. These stories, nevertheless, had two results. They aroused the Americans to demand revenge and they caused great resentment among the Indians who stoutly denied their truth.

The story of the "massacre" made an impression far and wide. A Scottish poet, Thomas Campbell (1777–1844), best known for his literary ballad "Lord Ullin's Daughter," in 1809 wrote a long narrative poem entitled *Gertrude of Wyoming*. In it there is reference to "the Monster Brant," although the Indian leader was nowhere near Wyoming at the time. The poem concerns the heroine Gertrude, her father Albert, and the hero, Henry Waldegrave. Henry lives in Albert's home for three years and later comes back to Wyoming and marries Gertrude. Shortly after they are wed, the attack on the settlement takes place and both Gertrude and Albert are killed. Young Henry then goes off to join Washington's army. In Campbell's biography in the *Dictionary of National Biography*, it is said of the poem that "despite manifest shortcomings, its gentle pathos and its general elegance and finish of style obtained for it a warm welcome."

The attack on Cherry Valley followed much the same pattern as the devastation of the Wyoming Valley. This time the British force was under the command of young Walter Butler, now a captain in the Rangers. It is not clear who commanded the Indians, although probably it was Cornplanter. Joseph Brant was the leader of thirty Mohawks, and Little Beard was among the Senecas who made up the majority of the Indians. In all, there were 321 Indians, 150 Rangers, and 50 soldiers from a British regiment.

The fort at Cherry Valley had been constructed earlier in 1778 and was commanded by Colonel Ichabod Alden (1739–78) of Massachusetts, whose intentions were good but whose military ability was not great. He had about 250 soldiers, who were not adequately supplied with food or ammunition. Alden refused to let the settlers move into the fort for protection, but he allowed his officers to find quarters in homes in the settlement instead of living in the fort even though he had been warned of the coming invasion. The attackers had also been able to learn where Colonel Alden was staying, so their first move on the morning of November 11 was to assault that house. Alden was tomahawked and scalped as he tried to escape and all the rest of the soldiers were killed or captured. Little Beard and a group of Indians also killed all the civilians in the household, thirteen in number.

Although Butler wanted to attack the fort at once, the Indians preferred to loot the village. They set fire to houses, killed civilians without mercy, and took all the goods they could carry. They even burned the homes of some who were loyal to England, explaining they had to do it so the Patriots would not know there were Tories in their midst. One woman and her four children were killed. On the other hand, Brant saved the life of one woman and three children by marking them with his war paint to show they belonged to him. One raider was baffled when the Reverend Samuel Dunlap's wig came off just as he was about to scalp him. A Mrs. Campbell was taken prisoner and carried off by the Senecas who, when they got home, gave her to an Indian family to take the place of a deceased member. Her children were distributed among other families. Two years later she was allowed to leave the Senecas and eventually she rejoined her husband.

The raid ended with every house in Cherry Valley destroyed and only the fort left standing. The raiders withdrew, taking seventy or so prisoners with them. Reports on the number of casualties differ but it appears that sixteen soldiers and thirty-two civilians—most of the latter women and children—were killed. A report to a New Jersey paper at the time of the massacre said the victims were "most barbarously murdered." Walter Butler claimed he did his best to prevent the Indians from running amok, and it is said he never again participated in an expedition when the Indians were in the majority. The attack was, however, defended on the British side as a proper military action against a fort and a supply center. At least, it was the last such warfare of the year. Winter was approaching and the Indians must do their late fall hunting to lay in food for the cold season.

On the larger scene of revolution and international affairs, the year 1778 was, on balance, favorable to the Americans, but far from decisive. The most important event was not a battle but the sealing of an alliance with France. The French had been assisting the Patriots with supplies for some time, more to harrass their old enemy Great Britain than to achieve a victory for democracy in America. The Rebel victory at Saratoga in 1777 was a major reason why the French early in 1778 agreed to a formal alliance with the United States and in the spring sent a fleet to help the colonists. On the military side, 1778 was a year of stalemate. The British abandoned Philadelphia in June and on the way back to New York fought an indecisive battle with General Washington's army at Monmouth, New Jersey. In August a combined Franco-American attempt, with General Sullivan in command, failed to drive the British out of Newport, Rhode Island.

The British, unable to bring the war to a decision in New England or the Middle Atlantic area, turned southward, and on December 29, 1778, they captured Savannah, Georgia. A month later Augusta fell. The British decision to turn southward was based partly on their belief that the area contained many Tories who would take up arms on the side of their king. An American attempt to retake Savannah with the aid of a French fleet failed in September 1779. In this battle, Casimir Pulaski (c.1748–79), the Polish patriot who had come to America in 1777 to aid the revolutionary cause, was fatally wounded while leading a cavalry charge.

In the north, aside from Sullivan's expedition, the only action in 1779 centered on the lower part of the Hudson River valley. The British failed when they tried to capture West

Point at the end of May, and in July Brigadier General Anthony Wayne and his men successfully stormed the almost impregnable British fort at Stony Point, farther down the Hudson. In September John Paul Jones achieved a stirring American naval victory when in his smaller ship the *Bon Homme Richard* he defeated the British frigate *Serapis*, in one of the most ferocious naval battles ever fought. At the end of the campaigning season of 1779, on October 17, Washington and his army went into winter quarters at Morristown, New Jersey, two days after General Sullivan's troops returned to Easton, from where they had started four months before.

During those four months they had been engaged in what was mostly guerrilla warfare, on both sides, against brave and tenacious warriors representing the most advanced and best organized of all North American Indians, the Iroquois.

"... the only savages capable of refined feelings"

The Iroquois Indians, who played so important a role in the early history of New York State and in the Revolution, were also known to the whites as the Six Nations. Their formal organization, the League of the Iroquois, was a unique confederation within Indian civilization.

Their origin is still not certain, but the Iroquois may have come north to the New York region from the south and southwest two hundred or three hundred years before the Europeans discovered America. On the other hand, there is some archeological evidence that they were in the northeast earlier and that their culture developed there over the centuries. By the time of the American Revolution, they occupied most of New York State, from the Hudson River on the east to the St. Lawrence River on the north, to Lake Erie on the west, but most of the Iroquois lived between the Hudson and Genesee rivers. The easternmost territory was that of the Mohawks, a strong, fierce tribe whose name meant "cannibals" or "maneaters." Next, to the west, lived the Oneidas, then the Onondagas, the Cayugas, and finally the Senecas, who guarded the western approaches to the confederacy and dwelled mostly east of the Genesee.

These made up the original Five Nations, which became six

in the first quarter of the eighteenth century when the Tuscaroras were admitted about 1715. They were a North Carolina tribe that suffered defeat at the hands of the whites and fled north. They were received into the Iroquois union but never quite enjoyed equal status with the others.

The exact date of the beginning of the League of Six Nations is lost in legend and by the lack of written records. One tradition says the league was formed in 1450, but this is probably about a century too early. If the beginning is to be dated to a particular year, 1570 is the one most often cited. It was some time after that, however, before the confederation became powerful and dominant in the northeast. Tradition also attributes the foundation of the league to one man, Hiawatha, but again various accounts do not agree in detail as to what took place. In some legends, Hiawatha is a Mohawk, in others an Onondaga. The poet Henry Wadsworth Longfellow added to the confusion with his long poem *Hiawatha*, published in 1855. Longfellow moved Hiawatha to the shores of Lake Superior, but did tell how he brought peace to warring tribes. The Iroquois Hiawatha was active around the middle of the sixteenth century.

In most versions of the story, Hiawatha was inspired to try to secure peace among the Iroquois tribes, which had been warring savagely with each other. In some accounts he did this by himself, but in most tales he is inspired and guided by Deganawidah. Deganawidah, in turn, is sometimes described as a saintly, heaven-inspired Indian, probably a Mohawk, sometimes as a god who revealed himself to Hiawatha and instructed him how to go about his task.

In the most elaborate version of the Deganawidah myth, Hiawatha, depressed by the constant warring of the tribes, which has resulted in the death of his wife and family, flees into the forest. Here the god Deganawidah, who was born of a virgin mother and who traveled across the lakes in a white stone canoe, came upon Hiawatha's cabin. From the roof he peered down through the smoke hole. Inside Hiawatha happened at that moment to be staring into a pot of water and saw the face of the god reflected in it. This, he felt, was not the face of an evil man and a cannibal, which he had become during his time in the forest.

At this moment Hiawatha was morally regenerated and the god revealed himself to him. He said the Indian must become his spokesman and the human being through whom his mission would be accomplished. Deganawidah had an impediment in his speech, even though he was a god, so Hiawatha was, literally, his spokesman. His eloquence, in going from one tribe to another, was such that all were prevailed upon to unite in peace. In some accounts it is said that Hiawatha was the only man who ever saw the god.

By the beginning of the eighteenth century, the governmental organization of both the individual tribes and the league was well developed. The confederacy was ruled by fifty sachems from the tribes. These positions were hereditary within the tribes, but not necessarily within the same family. No sachem could take his seat as a member of the league council until the whole body had invested him in a formal ceremony. The Mohawks and Oneidas were entitled to nine sachems each, the Cayugas ten, and the Senecas eight, while the Onondagas held the most sachemships—fourteen. As a body they exercised all the powers of government—executive, legislative, and judicial. The council usually met once a year, in the fall, at Onondaga. The Onondaga tribe, centrally located, was also the keeper of the council fire.

After the sachems in importance came the chiefs, selected within the tribes. There was no limit on the number of them, and the title was not hereditary. They were elected on merit. Both the sachems and the chiefs were civil officials, and if one of the former wanted to go on the warpath, he laid aside for the time his sachemship. Some of the chiefs were elected because of their military prowess, but the selection of leaders for waging war was mostly left to individuals who wanted to organize a war party. Later, to make sure any war effort of the

Six Nations was a united one, the sachems created two war-chiefships that were hereditary and both were assigned to the Senecas because on them fell the duty of fending off invaders from the west. Also, as time went on, chiefs who were leading warriors rose in importance in the affairs of the league. In fact, all the famous orators and wise men of the Iroquois came from among this kind of chief rather than the sachems whose positions gave them power and responsibility but little opportunity to stand out as individuals. Joseph Brant, for example, was a chief and the acknowledged war leader of the Mohawks in the Revolution, but he was never a sachem.

Although the Onondagas had the most sachems, each tribe, or nation, had an equal voice in making decisions. When they gathered at the council fire, the Mohawks, Onondagas, and Senecas sat on one side, for they were regarded as brothers to each other and fathers to the other nations. Thus the Oneidas and Cayugas, and later the Tuscaroras, were brothers to each other but children of the first three. The council of sachems allowed almost anyone to express his or her opinion on matters before it, and since there were no written records, ability as an orator was an important factor. The proceedings of the council were conducted with dignity and in good order, and all decisions had to be unanimous.

The Onondagas, as well as keeping the council fire, were also custodians of the pieces of wampum into which the Iroquois "talked" the laws of the league and the terms of treaties. Before the white men brought beads to America, wampum was made of mollusk shells strung on deer skin or sinew. By association in the mind of the man responsible, the designs worked into a piece of wampum enabled him to recite, when necessary, the terms of the treaty or other information indicated. Besides this ceremonial purpose, wampum was also used as money and for necklaces.

Although there are no reliable figures as to the total Iroquois population either before or at the time of the American Revolution, the Six Nations were not as numerous as tribes they conquered, especially the Hurons. Population estimates range as high as seventy thousand, but around 1650 there could not have been more than twenty-five thousand Iroquois and probably only about half that many. A hundred years later, as a result of the introduction of firearms and alcohol by the whites, the population had declined.

Despite their small population, the Iroquois, aided by the unity the league gave them and their unusual military prowess, created by conquest, between about 1600 and 1700, a sizable empire. At its greatest extent, it reached from the area of Canada around the eastern Great Lakes south to Tennessee and the Carolinas and westward to the Mississippi River. The Hurons, who occupied a large region in Ontario, who outnumbered the Iroquois, and who were allies of the French, were the main enemies of the Six Nations. In the early part of the seventeenth century the Hurons, with the Algonquins, carried on the bulk of the rich fur trade with the French in Canada. At that time they were powerful and numerous enough to feel they could treat the Iroquois with contempt. The Iroquois wanted to enjoy some of the benefits of the fur trade, especially after the Dutch came into upstate New York early in the century and entered the business.

Although the Hurons and the Iroquois negotiated over a number of years concerning rights in the fur trade, no settlement was reached, and bad feeling between the two groups grew worse. In 1648 the Senecas and the Mohawks attacked the Hurons. While the Iroquois won the first victory, the Mohawks were badly defeated when they tried to capture a Huron trading fleet near Montreal. The next year, in March, the two Iroquois tribes joined forces and, in an attack that took the Hurons completely by surprise, one thousand Iroquois warriors wiped out the town of St. Ignace. The appearance of such a deadly force in winter, when normally war parties stayed home, panicked the Hurons. Quite needlessly and heedlessly they abandoned fifteen villages almost at once. Between six and eight thousand of them crowded onto a small island with no food supply, and eventually most of them died. Others fled in other directions and within a year the strength of the once rich Hurons was broken.

The Neutral Nation, so-called because it stayed out of the war between the Iroquois and the Hurons, lived in southeastern Ontario, with the Niagara River on the east and Lake Erie to the south. Seeking an excuse to attack them, the Senecas and the Mohawks claimed among other points that the Neutrals had turned a Seneca over to the Hurons. In the summer of 1651, six hundred Iroquois attacked a town of the Neutrals that had a population of sixteen hundred. Everyone was killed, captured, or dispersed, and although the Neutrals were able to take one Seneca town, the war ruined them as a tribal unit. The Eries, who inhabited an area south and east of Lake Erie, their territory meeting that of the Senecas along the Genesee River, were attacked in 1656. The chief towns were taken and this tribe too was dispersed. A like fate overtook the Susquehannah Indians in 1675, and five years later six hundred Seneca warriors invaded the land of the Illinois Indians along the Mississippi River. So great was the fear of the Iroquois by that time that the Illinois abandoned their villages without a fight. At other times, the Iroquois attacked the Cherokees in Tennessee and the Catawbas in South Carolina, and ranged west and north into Michigan and to Lake Superior. When they conquered the Delawares they forbade them ever to go to war again and made all the men perform work such as agriculture, which they considered to be the women's task.

The arrival of the Europeans in America presented the Iroquois with an entirely new situation, one that was destined to change their way of life and, in the end, destroy their league and their civilization. The Iroquois' first contact with whites occurred in the sixteenth century when French fur traders and Jesuit missionaries entered their land. The Jesuits developed a feeling of admiration for the Iroquois and one of them wrote that, with the Hurons, they were "the only savages capable of refined feelings." The first great shock to the Iroquois resulting from the presence of these strangers occurred in 1609. Samuel de Champlain, the French explorer and the founder of Quebec, in that year led a party of French soldiers and Huron warriors south from Canada on an expedition that resulted in his discovery of the lake named for him. His party also met a force of Mohawks near present-day Crown Point, New York, and not only defeated them but also terrified them with firearms, which the Indians had never seen in use before.

The Iroquois, however, were in an advantageous position in relation to the white men. The latter were more than eager to acquire furs, especially beaver, and at the time of the Europeans' arrival in the New World, the area that became Canada and the northeastern United States abounded in fur-bearing animals. The Iroquois territory was some distance away from the French settlements in Canada, but near enough the water route the fur trade followed to make it vulnerable to their attacks. When the Dutch set up a fur trading post at Fort Orange (Albany) in 1614, the Iroquois could trade directly with them and could play the opposing whites off against each other. After the English ousted the Dutch from New York in 1664, the opposing sides became the French and Hurons against the British and the Iroquois. About this time, also, two new factors affected the situation. The intensive search for furs for the European market had resulted in the exhaustion of the supply in Iroquois territory and other nearby places so that trappers, both white and Indian, had to seek pelts further west. Also, the trade rivalry between the white nations led them to try to outdo each other in the goods they offered the Indians. As a result, the Indians were consuming too much alcohol and were becoming dependent on European goods, such as tools and fabrics.

In the early eighteenth century the Iroquois, with the British as allies, were at the height of their power, even though the seeds of future trouble had already been sown. The

Iroquois were flattered in 1710 when the British took some of their leaders to England where they met Queen Anne, who gave them four Bibles, a prayer book, and a set of communion plate for a Mohawk chapel that she had ordered built. Among the Indian visitors was John Brant, who was probably Joseph Brant's grandfather. With the final victory of the British later in the century in the French and Indian War, the winners became less dependent on their Indian allies than before, but the Iroquois remained faithful until the Revolution altered the situation again.

The Iroquois homeland, at the time the Europeans appeared, was almost entirely forested, and the Indians lived in small villages built near rivers or lakes in order to have a water supply. Almost the only open land was that which they cleared for agriculture. Boundaries between the lands of the different nations were quite definite by agreement. The many rivers and lakes provided low ground along which trails ran. The central trail ran through the land of all Six Nations, starting at the Hudson River and following generally the Mohawk River westward to the valley of the Genesee. It ended at the mouth of Buffalo Creek on the site of the city of Buffalo. From Oswego on the shore of Lake Ontario near its eastern end to Lewiston on the Niagara River ran the Ontario trail. It followed a ridge that is three to six miles inland and level most of the way. There were many other branch trails running north and south. The Indian trails were so obviously the best routes that later roads followed them very closely. The Iroquois tribes used trained runners to carry messages. Usually it took three days to get a message from the Hudson to Lake Erie but an exceptional runner could cover a hundred miles in a day. Sometimes relays of runners were used.

The Iroquois thought of themselves as "the people of the longhouses," with the Mohawks at the eastern door and the Senecas the "keepers" of the western door. They did, in fact, live in their villages in longhouses—a small village consisting of only one such building while some large villages contained more than a hundred. A longhouse was built by putting poles in the ground four or five feet apart and covering the structure with bark. There was a door at each end and smoke holes in the roof at intervals of about twenty feet. Longhouses were usually from fifty to one hundred thirty feet in length, and about sixty feet in width. Each two families shared a fire, so longhouses accommodated a number of families. Shelves along the walls provided benches by day and beds at night. Toward the end of the eighteenth century, when they had acquired metal tools, the Iroquois began to build individual log cabins like those of the white settlers. For many years Iroquois villages were surrounded by log stockades, but as their power grew and the danger from attack lessened, these were abandoned or made only strong enough to keep out wild animals.

The six tribes were the political units that operated through the league, while the social units were the clans, of which each tribe had eight, at least in theory. The eight clans were in two groups: Wolf, Bear, Beaver, and Turtle, who were brothers; and Deer, Snipe, Heron, and Hawk, who were also brothers. In addition, a Mohawk of the Wolf tribe considered himself the brother of a Seneca Wolf. Within the clans women had the dominant place and tribal government was a matriarchy. A man could not marry within his own clan, and when he married he went to live with his wife's clan. Children belonged to their mother's clan. When a chief died he could not pass his title to his son because the son was not of the same clan. Thus the women within the clan had the power to appoint new chiefs and even to depose chiefs who did not perform their duties properly. Husbands and wives kept title to their own property.

Both men and women took pride in their clothes. Before the white man came, clothing was made of skins, and the women skillfully and attractively decorated their skirts and jackets with materials such as porcupine quills. They also wore blankets as shawls. Jewelry, especially that made of silver, was much admired. After European materials became available, dresses were made of cloth and beads were used for decoration. Men wore breechcloths, shirts, leggings, and moccasins.

Agriculture and hunting and fishing were the chief occupations of the Iroquois, apart from warfare. Agriculture was left chiefly to the women, although the men did the first heavy work of clearing land to be tilled and might help with the harvest. Since the dog was the only domesticated animal, th Iroquois had no draft animals for plowing. As a result, this work had to be done by the women with implements of wood, stone, and shells. When they went to the fields they took the babies with them, strapped to their backs on flat boards. The babies were then usually placed under a tree and left to themselves while their mothers toiled. Corn, domesticated and cultivated by American Indians long before Europeans came to America, was the most important crop. Also raised were pumpkin, squash, and beans. Corn was pounded into flour and much of it dried and roasted for use during the winter. The Indians made maple sugar, and an early French explorer wrote that he had been served a new delicacy: popcorn with maple syrup on it. Nuts were an important food and hickory and chestnut were favorites. Acorns were eaten after boiling or roasting. The Iroquois grew tobacco, which they smoked but did not chew.

Hunting was an exciting sport as well as a necessary occupation to secure food. The main hunting season was the late fall and into the early part of the winter when the Indians tracked down deer, elk, moose, and bear. They also hunted wild fowl. With the aid of snowshoes, an Indian invention, the Iroquois could hunt in the winter. The Indian snowshoe was made by bending a piece of hickory wood to form a frame about three feet long and sixteen inches wide. Across the frame a network of deerskin strings was woven. Bows and arrows accounted for most of the game, but traps were also used. Spring was a good time for fishing.

"... the only savages capable of refined feelings"   29

Having no metals until the seventeenth century, the earlier Iroquois were dependent on fire and stone chisels for producing the weapons and other artifacts they needed. The Iroquois were competent potters and the ceremonial pipes they produced are especially impressive. They made war clubs and tomahawks with stone blades. The women were skilled in weaving baskets of different shapes and sizes for particular purposes. The Indians could tan the skin of animals they killed, having discovered that deer brains provided a satisfactory tanning agent. The soft and comfortable moccasin was made from a single piece of deerskin. And, of course, the Indians impressed the white men with their canoes, made from one piece of bark. Birch was preferred, but this tree was scarce in the Iroquois' lands.

Although the Iroquois had to labor hard to produce a living with their limited technology, they found time for games and put great enthusiasm into them. A bat with a webbing of skin at the end was the equipment used in a game that was the forerunner of lacrosse. Two teams vied in carrying, or knocking, the ball across the other's goal. Another game of skill called for the participants to try to throw a javelin through a rolling ring. Foot races were popular and so was archery, which provided not only a contest of skill but training for hunting and warfare. The Iroquois bow was three and a half to four feet long and it took great muscular power to draw the string back. The arrow was about three feet in length and feathered at the end in such a way as to make it revolve in flight, thus adding to the accuracy that could be achieved. The Iroquois were also fond of games of chance. In one of these, eight buttons made of elk horn and burned on one side to blacken them were tossed by contestants in turn. The object was to turn up as many buttons of the same color as possible and the Indians wagered enthusiastically on such games of chance.

Dancing was highly regarded among the Iroquois, both for worship and for pleasure. They had thirty-two dances in all, some patriotic, some religious, some social. The feather dance, which was religious, and the war dance, which was patriotic, were the two most important. Both were performed in costume and by selected groups of fifteen to twenty-five dancers. The war dance was a way of enlisting in a military expedition. It was usually performed in the evening with singers and drummers participating who offered a number of songs, each about two minutes long. A war whoop was given before each song. As with Indian dances in general, the dancing was chiefly upon the heel, which was raised and brought down very quickly and forcefully. The feather dance was more graceful than the war dance and also included a number of songs, all of them with a religious meaning.

The Iroquois believed in one god, the Great Spirit, who created and ruled the world. They saw the Great Spirit as the source of all the blessings they received. There was also an Evil Spirit and other inferior spirits, such as that of the winds. Some were good and some bad, and most natural objects were considered to be under some protecting spirit. Tobacco was a way of communicating with the spiritual world; it was an incense by means of which petitions could be sent to the spirits. The Iroquois also believed in the immortality of the soul and the punishment of evil deeds after death.

Iroquois religious worship consisted of celebrating festivals, of which there were six observed at stated times. The first in the spring was the Maple festival to give thanks for the sweet syrup from the tree. Next came the Planting festival to ask the Great Spirit to bless the seed being planted. The Strawberry festival was a way of giving thanks for the first food products of the new season while the Green Corn festival was celebrated when the corn and other vegetables ripened in the summer. The Harvest festival was a general thanksgiving when all the harvest was in. Finally came the New Year's festival, about February 1 by the white man's calendar. This festival ran for seven days, while four were given over to the Green Corn celebration, and one day to each of the others.

The New Year's festival culminated in the sacrifice of "the White Dog," one selected because it had no other color and so was the Iroquois emblem of purity and faith. Although they observed these occasions as part of their religion, the Iroquois had no clergyman or priesthood. Each clan did, however, select men and women who became known as "Keepers of the Faith." It was their responsibility to make arrangements for the festivals and sometimes they acted as confessors or moral censors of the people.

Villages had False Face societies, groups that wore masks on occasions such as the festivals and took part in the ceremonies. They were also supposed to be able to drive out witches and to cure disease. The masks were of wood, the faces more than life-size, and the features distorted into fearsome expressions. The Iroquois recognized the existence of an unconscious element in the mind, thus anticipating Sigmund Freud, the father of psychoanalysis, by several centuries. They believed that wishes were fulfilled in dreams, but they also realized that dreams might hide the real wishes of a soul. They felt that, if possible, dreams must be acted out: if a man dreamed he gave a feast for his friends he should get up and do so. Older people were held in high regard and well cared for, while great respect was shown for the dead. At one time Iroquois burial custom called for placing the body in a grave in a sitting position, facing east. In another kind of funeral ceremony, the body was placed on a scaffold or in a tree and left there until only the skeleton remained. The bones were then taken to the family home or placed in a small bark house built for that purpose nearby.

On the warpath, the Iroquois fought two kinds of wars. One was of the blood-feud type in which a family or a clan sought revenge for the death of one or more of its members. The other was the formal warfare of the Iroquois against other tribes, for conquest and territory. It was made bloodier by the competition for the fur trade with the Europeans. The League of the Iroquois prevented war within its membership but tended to promote more warfare with outside tribes. The start of a war was heralded by striking a tomahawk painted red into the war-post of a village. Anyone could then organize a war party and gather recruits. When they went on military expeditions, the Iroquois warriors lived mostly on a mixture of corn flour and maple sugar that gave a great deal of nourishment per pound.

Until he became armed with the white man's weapons, the Indian warrior wore armor of wood slats held together with deerskin thongs. The bow and arrow was his main weapon, but he used short spears and war clubs when charging into the midst of the enemy. One of the Indians' tactics was to pretend to retreat and then to trap the enemy when he advanced. After they acquired firearms, the Indians abandoned the useless wooden armor and wore as little as possible, to cut down the noise they might make and so they could move quickly through forests. For a long time, however, the Indians were unable to repair the new weapons because they did not have the tools or the training to use them. At one time the Mohawks asked the whites to send a smith to live among them to repair weapons. They were also, of course, dependent on the whites for gunpowder.

The torture of prisoners of war was a common practice among the Iroquois, their friends, and their foes. Every Indian warrior knew that if captured while on the warpath he was most unlikely ever to see his own tribe again. The Indians never exchanged prisoners, although occasionally they released a warrior to show their admiration for his bravery. Some prisoners were fortunate enough to be adopted by their captors. This was a fairly common practice, a prisoner being taken into an enemy family to replace some member who, as likely as not, had been killed or captured. Such adoptees usually accepted the situation and became loyal members of the tribe. In some cases prisoners were adopted only after they showed their courage and endurance by running the gauntlet. The women and children of the village formed in two rows, each person armed with a whip. If the prisoner, running between the rows and feeling the lash at every step, was able to stay on his feet to the end, he was adopted. Otherwise death was his fate.

To the Iroquois, the act of torturing a prisoner until he died was a religious rite and a ceremony of human sacrifice. The process itself was even crueler than the harsh methods used in Europe to put criminals and heretics to death. The Indians, both those doing the torturing and the victim, looked upon the matter as a test of courage and fortitude in which the victim must show no pain or fear in order to uphold the honor of his tribe. Every conceivable method was used to inflict pain, but always with the intent of making the torture last as long as possible without the victim's dying. The warrior being tortured suffered by fire in several ways: by being made to walk barefoot through a fire or by having hot knives applied to his skin. His muscles were pulled out and pierced and his fingernails yanked out. Fingers were crushed, flesh shredded, and his scalp removed. The whole village, including women and children as well as the men, took part. When the victim finally died, his body was cut up, cooked, and eaten as part of a ritual feast.

The Iroquois had no written language and so their history and legends were handed down through an oral tradition that was strong and remarkably accurate, as has been verified by comparing the Indians' spoken account with other sources. The Six Nations all spoke the same language, but each in a different dialect. Some, like the Mohawk and the Oneida, were much like each other, while some dialects showed considerable differences. These differences in the spoken language, as well as the absence of written records, cause complications in deciding how to spell an Indian proper or place name in English. No standards were established in colonial or revolutionary times, so the same name is spelled several different ways in the writing of the period and well into the nineteenth century. Most Iroquois names seem long and hard to pronounce to the American eye and ear. Not only were some of them wrongly translated when anglicized but in many cases they were also shortened. The state of New York to this day is almost solidly covered with English versions of Iroquois names for rivers, lakes, villages, and other geographical features. The Indian names were all descriptive. To a Seneca, Lake Ontario was Ne-ah-ga Te-car-ne-o-di, "the lake at Ne-ah-ga," which was a Seneca village at the mouth of the Niagara River where it enters Ontario. The name Genesee originally referred to "the beautiful valley" rather than to the river itself.

Having no written history of their own, the story of the Iroquois has reached the present day through the writings of white men, and so invariably the tale is told from their point of view, which often has been either unfriendly or mistaken. The Iroquois have been attractive subjects, both in such fields as history and anthropology and in fiction. The first serious study of the Iroquois was undertaken by Cadwallader Colden (1688–1776) and published in 1727 as *The History of the Five Nations*. Colden was a physician, born in Ireland of Scottish parents, who came to Philadelphia in 1710 and moved to New York in 1718. He wrote a significant book on physics in 1745, and in 1760 he became lieutenant governor of New York under the British crown, holding the office until his death. In 1765, radicals protesting the Stamp Tax burned his official coach. His history of the Iroquois was a carefully researched book. Colden wrote that the Iroquois were "a poor Barbarous People, under the darkest Ignorance." This, however, was preliminary to his asking, "But what have we Christians done to make them better?" His answer was that "instead of Vertues we have only taught them Vices, that they were entirely free of before. . . ."

Lewis Henry Morgan (1818–81) earned the title "father of American anthropology" as a result of his interest in the Iroquois. Born in Aurora, New York, Morgan became a lawyer and also began his study of the Iroquois, whose days of grandeur and power were still well remembered in New York in Morgan's time. He established friendly relations with some of the remaining Iroquois, who probably numbered no more than four thousand by that time, and in 1847 was adopted by the Senecas. His book, *League of the Ho-de-no-sau-nee or Iroquois*, was published in 1851 and is considered the first scientific study of the American Indian. A later work, showing that the kinship system of the Iroquois was like that of other Indians, was a ground-breaking work on primitive society in general. The Iroquois have appeared in many books, from fiction such as James Fenimore Cooper's *Leather-Stocking Tales* in the first half of the nineteenth century, to serious modern appraisals such as *Apologies to the Iroquois* by the eminent literary critic Edmund Wilson in 1960.

When the American Revolution broke out, the Iroquois were faced with a new and, to them, baffling situation. They had thought of the white men in New York State as one united group, all cheerfully living under the rule of the great king across the Atlantic. Now the white brothers were fighting each other and each faction was asking the Iroquois to side with it. The Indians were at this time entirely dependent on the whites for their supplies of many kinds and had to continue to get these goods from one or both sides. The British had a long and successful experience behind them in their dealings with the Iroquois. It had cost them considerable sums to hold the friendship of the Iroquois and they had found this expense worthwhile. The Americas on the revolutionary side were not used to dealing with the Indians on a diplomatic and business basis. They suddenly discovered they would have to do so and would have to assume the kind of obligations the British sustained if they wanted the neutrality or the help of the Iroquois.

In July 1775, the Continental Congress named commissioners to negotiage with the Indian population in the three sections of the colonies, north, central, and south. The commissioners for the northern department called the Iroquois to a meeting in Albany, which opened on August 25. The Americans spent considerable time trying to explain to the Indians why they were right in attempting to overthrow the government of King George III. The Indians drank the colonists' rum and ate their food while they deliberated. On August 31 they informed the commissioners that the six Nations would stay neutral. As Little Abraham, a Mohawk sachem said, it was a "family quarrel" and they would "sit still and see you fight it out." The Iroqouis, however, specified that the Americans must keep the war away from their territory or their neutrality would come to an end. To the Americans at the time, the decision for neutrality meant that the planned invasion of Canada could proceed without fear of Indian attack. Before too long, though, American actions upset the Indians. Some of the colonists killed some Mohawks, and the Iroquois were also upset by the treatment of Sir John Johnson, who was forced to agree not to fight the Rebels on pain of imprisonment. In addition, there were Iroquois not present at the Albany meeting who disagreed with the decision taken there.

The Indians in 1776 requested another meeting in Albany, which was held in late April, but with no representatives from the Senecas present. Little Abraham again spoke for the Indians and complained that the Americans were not supplying enough cloth and ammunition. At the end of the conference, neutrality was reaffirmed and the Indians received presents of gunpowder, lead for bullets, and cloth. Also, twenty-one of them were invited to go to New York to meet General Washington and to visit the leaders of Congress in Philadelphia.

The British worked constantly to get the Iroquois to fight on their side, and they, too, had some success. They held a secret council with the Six Nations at Niagara in September 1776, at which Cornplanter, Red Jacket, and Handsome Lake were present. The Seneca, Cayuga, Onondaga, and Mohawk tribes were here prevailed upon to take the side of the king. At another council at Oswego, representatives of these four tribes met again in January 1777 to hear the British urge them to take up arms against the Patriots. Joseph Brant, who was present at this meeting, argued for such a move, but was opposed by Cornplanter and Red Jacket. Brant prevailed, but by a majority vote, not by unanimous agreement. It was not long before some of them were fighting for the British, as at the Battle of Oriskany in August.

The Oneidas and the Tuscaroras, who followed the Oneidas' lead, refused to join the British side and, at the conference in Albany in September 1777, voted to support and fight for the Americans. In their terms they "accepted the hatchet." The Oneidas supplied guides to General Sullivan in 1779. Their decision to break with the rest of the original five nations came about largely through the influence of one man, Samuel Kirkland (1741–1808). Born in Connecticut, Kirkland became a missionary to the Iroquois when in his twenties. In 1766 he settled among the Oneidas, adopted their way of life, and served them for forty years. After the Revolution, in 1793, he founded a school in which he hoped white and Indian youths would be educated together. Few Indians attended, however, and, as Hamilton College, the school changed over to the usual college curriculum.

The quarrel between the Loyalists and the Patriots was reflected in the life of the Six Nations. They, too, became a house divided, fought each other on behalf of king or colonists, and, as a result, fragmented and destroyed the unusual power and prestige they had had before they became involved with western civilization.

"... total destruction and devastation"

Even before the worst of the British-Indian raids on the frontier settlements of New York and Pennsylvania in 1778, the Continental Congress, on the recommendation of its Board of War on June 10, voted the sum of $932,743, a large amount for the time considering the restricted resources of the Congress, to put down the Indian menace. This appropriation was intended to pay for a campaign against Detroit, a British strong point, and the Indians in that area, as well as against the Iroquois.

It was not possible to launch the campaign against the Iroquois in 1778, but in December General Washington recommended that it be planned for 1779, even at the expense of other possible offensive actions that year. Washington had also considered making an attempt to drive the British from some of their strong points on the Atlantic seaboard or launching another invasion of Canada. The Continental Army was not large or strong enough to undertake three offensives, and Washington in the end recommended a defensive stance for the most part in 1779, with comparatively large military power allotted to the Indian campaign. Congress approved Washington's plans on February 25, 1779, directing him to take all measures necessary to protect the settlers and to punish the Indians.

The expedition as planned had other purposes than simply punishing the Indians and protecting the pioneer Patriots. The

Indians and the Loyalists were supplying quantities of food to the British army, and if successful the expedition would reduce, if not cut off, this source. At the same time, Patriot farmers were producing food that went to the Continental Army and it was vital that the Indians be prevented from interfering with this supply. If the offensive achieved its ultimate aims, the strong points of Niagara and Oswego also would be taken, and British power, which had been seeking to link its forces in central New York with the regular army in New York City and elsewhere in the east, would suffer a considerable setback. Behind these immediate purposes lay another long-range goal that Washington especially was well aware of. The Revolution as a military operation was stalemated at this time, but events such as the French alliance were tipping the scales in favor of the Americans. It was likely only a matter of time until the British would have to grant independence to the colonies, but they would certainly give up only as much land as the Americans actually conquered by armed force. Washington knew from personal experience in the French and Indian War the potential value of the virgin lands in western New York, Pennsylvania, and other areas to the south and west. It was vital to conquer as much of this as possible before the Revolution ended if the United States was to amount to more than a strip of coastal territory.

These larger issues concerning peace treaties and the future of the nation were not, however, mentioned in Washington's specific orders concerning the expedition when he issued them to General Sullivan on May 31, 1779. The general wrote:

> This expedition you are appointed to command is to be directed against the hostile tribes of the Six Nations of Indians with their associates and adherents. The immediate objects are the total destruction and devastation of their settlements and the capture of as many prisoners of every sex and age as possible. It will be essential to ruin their

crops in the ground and prevent their planting more.

The expedition, in fact, would be primarily against the Senecas, rather than the other tribes of the Six Nations, and such British forces as might join in trying to turn back the Americans. In attacking the Senecas, the Americans would be facing the most advanced and most feared tribe among the Six Nations. The Senecas also occupied more territory than any of their brother tribes and were the largest in population, accounting, perhaps, for nearly half the people of the league. They were not only feared but respected by their enemies and they produced more remarkable men than the other five tribes.

The preparations for the expedition showed that Washington and the other leaders involved did not underrate the enemy. It was one of the most carefully planned campaigns of the war. Experienced officers were selected and the troops were well-trained Continentals. Most of them were veterans, although Indian fighting would be new to almost all of them and the land they were to invade was unknown country. The command of the expedition was first offered to General Horatio Gates (c.1727–1806) who was a native of England and who had fought in the British army in the French and Indian War. He joined the Patriots' side in the Revolution and in 1777, replacing General Philip Schuyler in command of the army facing General Burgoyne, brought the Saratoga campaign to a successful conclusion. Gates, however, declined the offer.

Washington had already decided that if Gates did not want the command it would go to Major General John Sullivan (1740–95). Sullivan was born on February 17, 1740, in the parish of Summersworth, New Hampshire. His father was a schoolmaster, who, with Sullivan's mother, emigrated from Ireland in 1731. Sullivan married in 1760, about the same time he finished studying law, and moved to Durham in 1763 where he was the first lawyer in the town. Although not tall, Sullivan had an erect bearing, black hair, piercing dark eyes, together with a dark complexion but ruddy cheeks. His fellow townsmen considered him overambitious, as he seemed greedy to acquire property and was quick to sue anyone who owed him money. He became a successful lawyer and acquired a good deal of land.

Sullivan entered public life, becoming a member of the first provincial congress of New Hampshire and one of that colony's two delegates to the first Continental Congress in the fall of 1774. Back home late in the year, he had his first military adventure as a major of militia who led an assault on Fort William and Mary at Portsmouth where, without bloodshed, the Patriots seized a considerable store of gunpowder. In 1775 he served in the second Continental Congress, and when that body selected officers for the Continental Army, beginning with George Washington as commander in chief, Sullivan was one of a number of brigadier generals chosen.

Serving under Washington and in command of a brigade at the siege of Boston, Sullivan on August 26, 1775, led a force that seized a hill and held it against a British attack. He was not so successful on December 29 when he failed to take some buildings and barracks on Bunker Hill from the British. Sullivan's behavior in the army soon came in for criticism. He was extremely patriotic, loyal to Washington, and almost recklessly brave, but he was overly ambitious, arrogant, and so sensitive to any adverse comments that he was often involved in controversies.

Late in May 1776, Washington sent Sullivan north toward Canada with six regiments to assist the American forces there. This army was in no condition for further battle, having been defeated in December, and was suffering from mismanagement and a smallpox epidemic. On arrival in Canada, Sullivan found that Brigadier General John Thomas had died, and so he assumed command. By mid-June Sullivan decided correctly that he had no choice but to order a retreat back to the colonies, which he carried out successfully. Nevertheless, it was a retreat, and when he got back he found that Congress had promoted Horatio Gates to major general and would have put him in command in Canada had an army remained there. Touchy as ever, Sullivan therefore offered his resignation but later was permitted to withdraw it.

Sullivan felt more satisfied with his lot when he, too, was promoted to major general in August and chosen by Washington to replace the ailing Major General Nathanael Greene in command of American troops on Long Island where they were preparing to face the large invasion force of General Howe. When the British attacked on August 27, Sullivan's force held the American left wing. The British surprised the Americans with an attack that hit the left flank and its rear. Sullivan's force was crushed, his men fled, and the army and Sullivan suffered a shattering defeat. For a while Sullivan and about four hundred men put up a stubborn resistance, but in the end the general had to surrender. Some officers blamed Sullivan for the American defeat and he does deserve some censure, but the overall reason for the loss was the inexperience of the Patriot generals and soldiers compared with that of the disciplined, professional British regulars.

Sullivan was well treated by General Howe, who insisted he was anxious to make peace with the Americans. Sullivan was paroled to go to Philadelphia to carry this message to the Patriots' leaders there. This he did, but Congress did not believe that Howe either could or would grant terms that would be satisfactory to them. Once again, Sullivan was criticized. His intentions were good and he had no thought of deserting the American cause, but he was naive to believe that independence could be achieved in this way. Shortly after this incident Sullivan was exchanged for a British prisoner and rejoined the army.

He was more fortunate in his next encounter with the British. Washington put him in command of several brigades that formed one part of the attack on Trenton, New Jersey, on a cold, icy December 26, 1776. Sullivan and the men under him performed well and did their share in winning a solid victory, the first Sullivan had enjoyed. Sullivan again did well on January 3, 1777, at the Battle of Princeton, where he commanded one of the Americans' main units. His part in the victory showed him to be a brave fighter and a determined leader.

Sullivan did not, however, continue to enjoy success. At the Battle of Brandywine, in southeastern Pennsylvania, on September 11, 1777, he commanded the American right. The British feinted elsewhere but threw their main attack at Sullivan's troops who were threatened from both front and rear, much as they had been on Long Island. The American army was soundly defeated and Sullivan once more came in for a great deal of criticism. He did not perform his task as well as he might have, but he was not the only American leader who made mistakes that day. Washington next decided to attack the British army at Germantown, about five miles from Philadelphia. The battle began on the morning of October 4, which turned out to be a foggy day that hampered the movements of the troops and made it difficult to know what was going on at any distance. Sullivan commanded the right wing and Washington accompanied him, leaving General Greene in charge on the left. Sullivan's force surprised the enemy and for a while drove the British back and advanced into Germantown. Just when victory seemed possible, other troops on Sullivan's left flank began falling back and two American units, in the fog and the smoke from the guns, each thought the other was British and began firing on their own men. Perhaps Sullivan could not have gone further anyway because the British were rallying and the Patriots were about out of ammunition. Sullivan's men began to retreat after they learned others were already doing so. As usual, there were uncomplimentary insinuations in some quarters about Sullivan's conduct, but Washington spoke up in his defense.

Hardly had Sullivan returned from the Germantown battlefield before he had to face a court of inquiry established to look into his conduct of a raid on Staten Island, in New York harbor, which he had planned and commanded on August 22. The British had troops on the island who raided the New Jersey coast to the west, seizing some cattle. Sullivan's men struck at the British at two points, and as with some other Sullivan operations, all went well at first. The British, however, began striking back and the Americans did not maintain discipline. The return by boat to New Jersey ended in chaos, and the rear guard had to surrender. The court of inquiry on October 12 decided, however, that the raid had been well planned and that the disaster that overtook it was not Sullivan's fault.

Although he was exonerated, Sullivan was still much upset by the whole incident because he felt, and with justification, that some of those who demanded the inquiry simply disliked him and wanted to force him out of the army. Sullivan wrote a letter to the president of Congress in which he angrily asserted that the action against him was "a poor Encouragement to Sacrifice that Life which I have often ventured in my Countrys Cause & to Exchange Domestick Ease for the Dusty field of Mars." Congress saw the justice of Sullivan's case and resolved that the action of the inquiry in absolving him was pleasing to it.

Sullivan was one of the loyal band of officers and men who suffered through the winter of 1777–78 at Valley Forge, about twenty miles from Philadelphia, with George Washington. Here the army in its winter quarters held on in spite of a shortage of food and warm clothing. Sullivan was put in charge of building a bridge over the Schuylkill River. When that task was finished he asked Washington for leave to go home and attend to his personal affairs for a while. The commanding general refused but on March 10, 1778, offered Sullivan the command of the American forces in Rhode Island, which he accepted.

The British held Newport at this time, and the Americans

wished very much to dislodge them from that important seaport. The opportunity seemed to have arrived with the coming to American waters in July of a strong French fleet, which also carried troops and was commanded by the Comte d'Estaing. The French admiral would approach Newport from the sea and land his troops while Sullivan led his soldiers down from the north. At first the plan worked well, but Sullivan, hot tempered as always, quarreled with the French commanders. Quite likely he had some justification, but that did not help matters. Then a British fleet appeared and d'Estaing, in the midst of disembarking the French troops, took them back on board and put out to fight the British ships. At sea, a wild storm damaged and scattered both fleets so that neither was in any condition to fight. D'Estaing sailed to Boston to repair his ships. This left Sullivan facing the British alone and nearly surrounded in the northern part of the island on which Newport is located. Eventually, after putting up a gallant defense, the Americans were able to withdraw safely and avert disaster. Once again Sullivan had failed, but once again it seemed that luck was against him.

Sullivan played no further part of consequence in the war until March 1779, when Washington offered him the overall command of the campaign against the Iroquois. On May 7 Sullivan arrived in Easton, where the major force of the expedition was to be organized and which would be the jumping-off place for the march northwest into New York. The campaign was, however, to be a three-pronged affair. The second part was to consist of a considerable force that would form at Otsego Lake (the Glimmerglass of Cooper's novels) in east central New York and move south on the Susquehanna River to join Sullivan at Tioga in northern Pennsylvania. The third and smallest force would assemble at Fort Pitt, go up the Allegheny River to the Genesee country and meet the rest of the expedition there.

The units of the expedition scheduled to meet Sullivan at Tioga were commanded by Brigadier General James Clinton

(1733–1812), born in New York State and a member of a family prominent in the state's affairs. His brother George was governor in 1779, while his son De Witt was a future governor as well as the builder of the Erie Canal, constructed between 1817 and 1825. James fought in the French and Indian War and served in the disastrous American campagin in 1775 against the British in Canada. He commanded Fort Clinton, on the Hudson near Kingston, in 1777 when Sir Henry Clinton and the British army sought to advance up the river and join forces with Burgoyne. Clinton led a heroic defense of the fort and suffered a bayonet wound, but the British overpowered his troops. He participated in the last battle of the Revolution at Yorktown, Virginia, in 1781.

General Clinton led his brigade, totaling about fifteen hundred men, out of Schenectady early in June 1779. The men traveled in 212 boats on the Mohawk River. These were built for the campaign, and at Canajoharie they had to be taken out of the river, loaded onto wagons, and transported twenty miles over hills to Otsego Lake. Before this move Clinton made Canajoharie his headquarters for several weeks and while he was there had two Tories executed as spies and one American deserter shot.

Colonel Daniel Brodhead commanded the force that was to move north from Fort Pitt. He left that western Pennsylvania outpost on August 11 with 605 officers and men, and he had one month's provisions, which were sent by boat up the Allegheny. Brodhead also took along some Delaware Indians as scouts, as well as livestock and pack horses. The only brush with enemy Indians that Brodhead had took place when an advance guard of soldiers and Indians came upon a Seneca scouting party of thirty or forty warriors traveling by canoe. There was a brief exchange of shots, several of the Senecas were killed, and the rest fled. After that, the Indians disappeared into the forest when Brodhead's men came near. He destroyed the deserted villages he found, although in at least one the Indians had time to collect their corn and other possessions and bury them so the Americans could not find them. In all, Brodhead estimated that his men destroyed about five hundred acres of corn and other vegetables. They also secured a large amount of plunder, which, when they got back to Fort Pitt, their commander had sold and the proceeds divided among the men.

It is impossible from the records to tell just how far north Brodhead got, but probably he crossed the boundary between Pennsylvania and New York and reached the vicinity of the later small city of Salamanca, some sixty-odd miles southwest of the point at which Sullivan crossed the Genesee, before turning back. Sullivan and Brodhead sent messengers to each other, but neither ever secured any information in time to help in planning a meeting of their troops. As a result, the two forces never joined as scheduled and the Brodhead unit was back in Fort Pitt on September 14, returning by a different route from the one taken going north. By that time his men were mostly shoeless and short of clothing, or "barefoot and naked" as Brodhead put it. He also said they had returned with the loss of neither "man or beast." The officers and men had been much impressed by the prosperity of the Indians and the extent of their villages. "The greatest part of the Indian houses were larger than common," Brodhead wrote to Washington.

General Sullivan spent nearly a month and a half, from May 7 to June 18, at Easton, assembling his army and gathering supplies before he felt ready to undertake the first stage of the march to Wyoming. Among the equipment and supplies were 4,285 horseshoes, 254 spades, 385 shovels, and 100 candlesticks. One regiment asked that it be issued 325 tomahawks.

Sullivan also gathered the officers who would command the brigades and regiments making up the army. Besides General Clinton, who was coming from the north, the brigades were led by Brigadier Generals Hand, Maxwell, and Poor. Edward Hand (1744–1802) was born in Ireland and emigrated to

Philadelphia in 1767. He participated in the siege of Boston, fought with gallantry in the Battle of Long Island, and in 1778 was in command of troops at Albany. William Maxwell (1733–96) was also born in Ireland and came to the United States about 1747. He joined a British regiment in the French and Indian War and was with General Edward Braddock's army in 1755 when it suffered a crushing defeat near Fort Duquesne (later Fort Pitt) at the hands of the French and their Indian allies. Maxwell served under Sullivan in 1775, fought in the Canadian campaign and at Brandywine and Germantown. Of Scotch-Irish descent, he was known as "Scotch Willie" because of his accent. Enoch Poor (1736–80) was born in Massachusetts, entered the American army in 1775, and took part in the siege of Boston and the fighting at Trenton and Princeton. He was reported to have fought well at Saratoga and after the Sullivan campaign was commended for his "intrepidity and soldiery conduct."

Colonel Thomas Proctor was in command of the expedition's artillery, the First Pennsylvania regiment. The artillery consisted of four brass three-pounders (which fired balls of the weight indicated); two six-pounders; two five-and-a-half-inch howitzers (which had shorter barrels and fired their projectiles in a higher, more arching manner than other cannon); and one cohorn. The cohorn was a small gun with four short legs. It could be carried easily, and the legs allowed it to sit quite firmly on rough ground. It turned over backward every time it was fired so the soldiers called it the "grasshopper."

Typical of regimental and other unit commanders were Colonels Willett, Dearborn, Cilley, and Dayton. Marinus Willett (1740–1830), born in New York State, fought in the French and Indian War like so many of his generation and joined the American army in the Revolution. He took part in the Canadian campaign, but his finest accomplishment was at the siege of Fort Stanwix in 1777. As the Battle of Oriskany was being fought nearby, Willett led a sortie with 250 men from the fort. He raided the British camp, destroyed many supplies and returned to the fort with little loss. This was one of the events that discouraged the British and the Indians so that they abandoned the siege. From 1780 to the end of the war, Willett led troops in the Mohawk Valley and it was his men who killed Walter Butler in 1781. Late in his career Willett was mayor of New York City in 1807–8.

Henry Dearborn (1751–1829) came from New Hampshire like his commander. He was at the Battle of Bunker Hill in 1775, was captured in the course of the Canadian expedition, but was exchanged. He was back in the American army during the Saratoga campaign and wintered at Valley Forge in 1777–78. Dearborn had a distinguished but controversial career in later life, serving as secretary of war in President Thomas Jefferson's cabinet. In the War of 1812, as a major general, he commanded the northern frontier from Niagara to the Atlantic Coast; but his inaction, which led to the British capture of Detroit, among other events, was strongly criticized, and he was relieved of his command in 1813. Fort Dearborn, out of which grew the city of Chicago, was named for him.

Joseph Cilley (1734–99) and Elias Dayton (1737–1807) were less well known than Willett and Dearborn, but both proved useful leaders in the campaign about to start. Cilley came from New Hampshire and Dayton from New Jersey, and they had much the same experiences in the Revolution as many others. Cilley took part in the siege of Boston, fought his way to safety through the British lines at the Battle of Long Island, and was in combat at Trenton and Princeton. Dayton took part in the British capture of Quebec in the French and Indian War, fought at Germantown in the Revolution, and suffered at Valley Forge with the Continental Army.

It was June 23, five days after the expedition left Easton, that it reached Wyoming, having averaged only about ten miles a day. An attempt had been made to build a road through hitherto unopened territory, but dense forests, rough and rocky terrain, and swamps made it difficult for an army, encumbered with supplies and equipment, to make good time.

(Swamp, incidentally, did not to these men necessarily mean an open area of water and reeds. In some places the ground was soggy enough to make walking difficult because the forest was so thick no sun penetrated to dry out the ground.) The missionary Samuel Kirkland joined the march on June 20. The next day the army entered the Great Swamp, "horrid rough gloomey country" that went on for twenty miles and resulted in "broken wagons and tired horses." After he reached Wyoming, one officer wrote home that the greater part of the march had been "through the most horrid swampy wilderness and barren mountain desert I ever saw."

Sullivan found more supplies awaiting him at Wyoming but also discovered that the salted meat was unfit to eat. In addition, he did not think the supply of shoes and clothing was adequate, and some of the cattle were in such poor condition they could not walk. Sullivan at once wrote to Washington reporting these things and also that the bread was moldy and the troops were not up to his expectations. "I have every possible disappointment and difficulty to grapple with. I will endeavor to surmount the whole, but I cannot look upon myself answerable for Consequences. . . ." All this meant that Sullivan would stay much longer in Wyoming than he had planned, and so the expedition would be badly delayed in getting about its serious business.

Meanwhile, he kept up his complaints to Washington and to Congress. He told the commanding general he did not think he and Clinton would have enough men by the time they reached the territory where fighting was likely because they would have to leave so many to guard the rear. Also, a force of 720 rangers from Pennsylvania had been promised but had not arrived. Washington, for his part, criticized Sullivan for wanting to accumulate too much in the way of provisions. Clinton, he told Sullivan, would have so many supplies and boats that there was no chance he could effect his junction with Sullivan secretly. When Sullivan wrote directly to John Jay as president of Congress, Washington took exception to his complaint that the supply system had failed and that he would not have enough soldiers.

The supply situation began to improve on June 29 when thirty-four boats arrived from Sunbury, Pennsylvania, carrying flour, beef, and military stores. A month later, on July 24, another 134 boats arrived from the same place. Four days later eighty wagons came in from Easton with provisions. Still unhappy, General Sullivan wrote on July 30 that he was resolved to march the next day even though he still had "scarcely a coat or blanket for every seventh man." He concluded gloomily, "A very severe campaign I expect we shall have."

The Wyoming area where the army had been awaiting the order to march was a pleasant place "through which," as one journal keeper wrote, "runs the Susquehanna, in a swift delightful course." He recognized the fertility of the land and said the river yielded many fish. The settlement itself, however, presented a sad and desolate air after the attack of the previous year. What had formerly been a prosperous settlement was in ruins, and Lieutenant Colonel Adam Hubley, writing of the "poor Inhabitants" in his journal, noted that "two thirds of them are Widdows and Orphans, who by the vile hands of the savages have been most cruelly deprived some of tender husbands and some Indulgent parents and others of affectionate friends & acquaintances, besides robb'd & plundered of all their furniture and Clothing."

The third anniversary of the Declaration of Independence on July 4 was observed appropriately, and Lieutenant Robert Parker commented in his journal, "The troops were paraded ... when thirteen pieces of Cannon were discharged." There was also "an excellent discourse ... delivered suitable to the occasion by the Rev'd Doct. Gans." Another account says that Kirkland and a Mr. Hunter also preached. The next day, General Hand gave a dinner at which thirteen toasts were drunk.

The routine life of an army went on, one journal (of a

considerable number that were kept, mostly by officers but some by enlisted men) recording under June 30 that "the men were employed in cleaning themselves and arms." The first taste of what was to come was reported on July 15: "The Indians skulking around our camp. Killed and scalped one man, who was driving up some horses and wounded another." Two days later, one man was "killed and scalped and one other wounded." The Iroquois spied on Sullivan's army from start to finish of the campaign and sent reports quickly back to their tribal leaders and to the British.

On the last day of July, about 1 P.M., the army finally left Wyoming for Tioga, its next goal, about eighty miles away. The total force of about three thousand included three chaplains, ten surgeons, eight drum majors, and three fife majors. Some one hundred men under the command of Colonel Zebulon Butler were left behind as a garrison to guard the base. Sullivan placed Hand's brigade in front, in three columns, and somewhat ahead of the main body. Maxwell's brigade marched on the left and Poor's on the right, with the twelve hundred pack horses and eight hundred cattle between them and behind them. One regiment served as a rear guard while scouts were out on both flanks to watch for any enemy activity. Colonel Proctor's artillery and some baggage traveled in 214 boats up the Susquehanna against the strong current. The army and the boats were supposed to stay abreast of each other and the boats were to sound horns regularly to show their position. Although the expedition tried to keep as compact a formation as possible, the nature of the terrain made this difficult. At times the line of march was six miles long, watched from the hills all the time by Indian scouts.

The first day's march covered only ten miles, which brought the army to Lackawanuck where it had to remain until the next day so that the struggling boats could catch up. Two of them were already lost. Slowly the army went on from day to day, reaching Wyalusing, about fifty-three miles from Wyoming, on August 5. As one soldier said of the land he marched

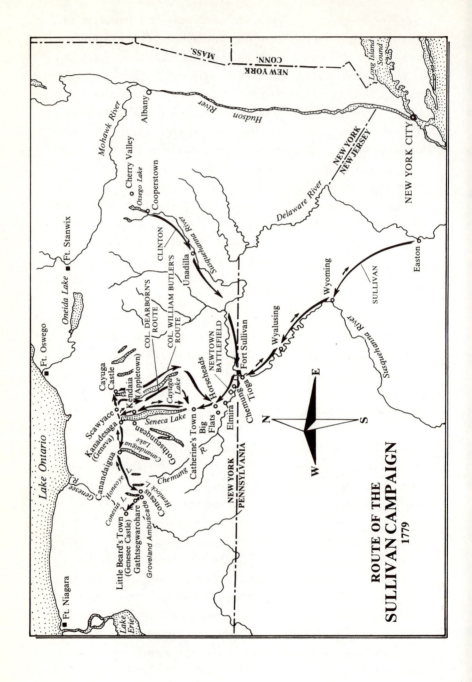

through, "It abounded chiefly in deer and rattlesnakes." While the expedition was at Wyalusing, Sullivan fell ill, and when the march resumed he traveled by boat until August 10, when he resumed command. During part of the march on August 9, the army had to use a path about a foot wide with a precipice of 180 feet on the left. Several pack horses and three cattle slipped off the path and were killed. The following day, Sergeant Major George Grant recorded in his journal simply, "Lay by on account of rain." This entry, and an even more laconic one, "Nothing material," alternated with Grant's rather colorful accounts of more exciting events. The expedition inflicted its first damage on the enemy on August 9 when an Indian village of about thirty houses was burned, but the inhabitants were gone.

On August 11 the army forded the Susquehanna, moving from the east to the west bank. Going on north the troops forded the Chemung River near where it flows into the Susquehanna, and so had reached their immediate goal, Tioga, meaning in Iroquois "at the forks." On the way that day they passed the ruins of Queen Esther's Castle, an Indian settlement that had been destroyed the previous year. The next day Sullivan ordered a fort, consisting of a stockade and four blockhouses, built at Tioga, on the narrow isthmus of land formed by the two rivers as they near each other. The march from Wyoming had been a hard one and several soldiers died of heat and exhaustion while another drowned.

About twelve miles up the Chemung lay the Indian town of that name, and Sullivan had heard that a force of Iroquois warriors might gather there. Accordingly, the general sent out a scouting party under Captain John Cummings to try to determine the number of Indians and whether they seemed to be preparing for battle. The scouting party was unable to decide what the enemy was up to, but one soldier who crept into the encampment estimated the number of the foe at seven hundred, which was probably too high.

Sullivan decided to attack in force with most of the army,

including one howitzer for which Colonel Proctor built a light carriage that made it possible to move the gun easily. On the morning of the thirteenth the American forces surrounded the village but found it deserted. The Indian warriors had moved north a mile or so and taken up positions there. The village of Chemung, consisting of about forty houses, was burned, and corn, variously estimated as covering from forty to sixty acres, was destroyed.

General Hand's brigade then proceeded up the river toward the enemy position. The men in advance were warned by those experienced in Indian warfare to beware of an ambush. In spite of the warning, the Indians were not discovered until they opened a heavy fire on the Americans. The affray has thus become known as the Chemung Ambush. Hand's men returned the fire and prepared to charge the Indian force, which, however, fled. Sullivan reported seven men killed and thirteen wounded. The Indian casualties, if any, were not known since they were not pursued and since they carried off their dead and wounded whenever possible.

General Sullivan next prepared to send part of his force north to meet General Clinton and escort him into Tioga.

"The troops were much animated"

On the day he left Wyoming, General Sullivan sent word by messenger to General Clinton to leave Otsego Lake on August 9. Clinton was already making his preparations, which called for an unusual use of the lake, eight miles long and about a mile wide. Otsego means "rock place" in Iroquois and was so called because of a particular rock at the outlet of the lake. This outlet, near Cooperstown, is the beginning of the Susquehanna River, which in all is 444 miles long and empties into Chesapeake Bay. Clinton planned to dam up the outlet to accumulate as much water as possible in the lake until he was ready to leave. Then the dam would be broken and the accumulated water would sweep obstructions out of the river and help speed his more than two hundred boats downstream.

While this work was going on, Sullivan wrote from Wyoming to Washington and expressed optimism, although he still did not think he had enough supplies to see him through the Indian country. And in this same period, Colonel John Butler, on the British side, heard of the arrival of the Americans at Tioga. He passed on word that the Six Nations were in a "disagreeable situation" and were worried as to "how to meet the rebels who were advancing on all sides."

Clinton opened his dam on August 9 and started the boats down the river while his force of fifteen hundred men marched overland. The flood caused by breaching the dam both surprised and frightened the Indians who took it as a bad omen. It destroyed some of their growing crops and could not be accounted for by any natural rainfall. The rising waters also surprised Sullivan's men farther down the river's course. On his march Clinton destroyed five Indian villages.

At Tioga on August 16, Sullivan sent out one thousand men under General Poor to meet Clinton and escort him to Tioga. The two forces met on August 19, and three days later Clinton and his men marched into the Tioga camp. They were greeted with a thirteen-gun salute and Colonel Proctor's band played to celebrate the occasion.

Major General Sullivan's army now consisted of four brigades made up of an assortment of units. Maxwell's first brigade had four regiments, all from New Jersey. Poor's second brigade also had four regiments, three of which were from Sullivan's home state, New Hampshire, while the other was the Sixth Massachusetts. The third brigade, commanded by Hand, consisted of eight assorted units. There were two Pennsylvania regiments, the German Battalion, Morgan's Riflemen, the Independent Rifle Company, the Wyoming Militia, and the Independent Wyoming Company. The last three were comparatively small units, commanded by captains. Hand also had under him the artillery regiment of Colonel Proctor. Clinton, who was second in command of the expedition, brought into camp six units, four of them New York infantry regiments. He also had under him the New York Artillery Detachment and the Volunteer Corps. The combined forces of Sullivan and Clinton made up an army of just about 4,500 officers and men fit for duty.

The combined force remained at Tioga until August 26, although the next stage of the march would have started a day earlier except for heavy rains. Three friendly Oneida Indians came into camp on August 25 and would serve as guides. Meanwhile, the soldiers were cutting up tents to make bags in which to carry flour, while Sullivan was arranging for a small garrison to remain at Tioga, to receive more supplies that might come up from Wyoming. In his honor, the military post here was named Fort Sullivan.

The Army marched out on August 26, heading northwest up the Chemung River to the Indian village of Newtown, about twelve miles distant and about five miles southeast of the modern city of Elmira. Here, the expedition had reason to believe, might be found a strong force of Indians and British. On this same day, Butler wrote to the commanding officer at Fort Niagara that Sullivan's army included "some of the best of the Continental Troops commanded by the most active of the Rebel Generals."

As before, this Rebel general had done a workmanlike job of arranging his forces for the march. Sullivan placed Hand's brigade in front, with Maxwell on the left and Poor on the right. Clinton's men took up the rear position. The march was not easy. The terrain was difficult enough to begin with and recent heavy rains added to the problem. The army made only about four miles the first day. As to the next day, one officer wrote that "there was several Indians saw on our March to day, but they made their escape." His entry for August 27 reported, "Very heavy Dew this morning did not move to day till 2 oClock occasioned by our Amunition waggons breaking Yesterday & had to mend them." Meanwhile, Sergeant Moses Fellows described August 27 as "much Impeded by the Artilery and amunition Waggons threw thick woods and Difficult Defiles, Such Cursing, Cutting and Diging, over seting Wagons.... we arrived at a large Place of Corn Containing about 80 Acres as Good as I ever beheld, with Great Quantities of Squashes Beenes &c...." The corn and other vegetables were destroyed. On August 28 the army neared Chemung and Sullivan sent out scouts to try to determine the enemy's position, strength, and intentions. The scouts reported that an enemy force was indeed about five miles away, near Newton. They also reported that they had heard the sound of axes and concluded the Indians and British were building some sort of defensive works. Sullivan decided to move to the attack the next day, but cautiously.

The army advanced toward the enemy beginning about 9 A.M. on Sunday, August 29. Some of Hand's men, who were again in front of the rest of the army, reported about two hours later that they had sighted enemy breastworks a mile or so in front of Newtown. This obstacle lay across the trail beside the Chemung, which followed essentially the same path as the modern New York State Route 17. The enemy had camouflaged the breastworks with trees and branches cut down the day before, but they were placed too regularly and some of the leaves were wilting so that the American scouts had little difficulty in detecting the ruse. Firing broke out on both sides while Hand waited for the rest of the army to arrive. The Indians for their part made frequent rushes from behind their barricade in an attempt to draw the Americans into their strong point.

The enemy's arrangement was intended to set a trap for the whole American army. The barricade ran north and south just beyond a creek the Americans would have to cross. On the right of the breastworks and to the rear was a ridge running mostly east and west with its far end nearly at the river. On this were Rangers and British troops who could fire on Sullivan's left flank if he tried to advance along the route blocked by the breastworks. On the left of these works the enemy position was protected by a swamp and by a steep hill. On the latter a force of Indians was in position to disrupt the Americans' right flank as the army advanced.

After holding a council of war, Sullivan determined on a plan of action to avoid being ambushed. Colonel Proctor's artillery was placed in position about three hundred yards in front of the enemy's breastworks, with Maxwell's brigade behind the guns in support and in reserve. Colonel Matthias Ogden and his First New Jersey regiment (part of Maxwell's brigade) were on Proctor's left, between him and the river, to cut off escape in that area and to prevent any attempt by the enemy to get around the American left flank. General Poor's brigade was ordered up the enemy northern, or left, flank. He was to be followed, behind and to his right, by Clinton's brigade. Finally, Hand's brigade would lead the advance against the enemy's center as soon as the artillery had weakened the fortification.

Allowing an hour for Poor to get in position, Sullivan ordered the artillery to open fire at 3 P.M. Poor, however, was unable to carry out his part of the plan on time because the very watery swamp, overgrown with brush, proved a formidable obstacle. The artillery opened up on schedule and quickly demoralized the Indian defenders. Explosive shells, bursting over their heads and behind them, made the Indians think they were surrounded and being fired on from the rear as well as the front. They broke and ran. As Lieutenant William Barton later described it, the shelling "caused them to give several yells, and doubtless intimidated them much." Hand's brigade swept through the center of the enemy line with little resistance, and this advance, in turn, forced the British on the ridge to the south to withdraw also lest they be cut off from their Indian allies.

The heaviest fighting took place in Poor's sector where his men had to wade through the swamp, cross a creek, and then fight their way up the rugged hill. Lieutenant Colonel George Reid and his Second New Hampshire Regiment bore the brunt of the action. They not only had to fight the enemy on the hill ahead but they also became involved with some of the Indians fleeing from the breastworks, who came upon Reid's regiment at its flank and rear. Reid was nearly surrounded when Colonel Dearborn, whose regiment was next to Reid's, came to his rescue. Meanwhile, the rest of Poor's men were fighting their way up the hill, the enemy putting up strong resistance. The Americans pressed on, and when the Indians there saw that they, too, were nearly surrounded, they joined the rest of their comrades in flight. The main American force pursued the enemy for a mile or so and some of the light corps went on for another mile but were unable to make further contact. A solid victory had been won, but because Poor was delayed in his march by the nature of the terrain, the opportunity of surrounding the British and Indians and inflicting crushing casualties was lost. The battle had taken about seven hours to fight.

Neither side suffered very many casualties, although there are contradictory reports as to the losses of the Indians. Sullivan, in a letter he wrote the next day to Washington, reported only three soldiers killed and thirty-nine wounded, mostly in Poor's brigade. At least one of the wounded died the day after the battle. John Butler wrote back to Niagara that the British and the Indians had a total of twenty-two casualties. He said five of the Rangers were killed or captured and three wounded, while five Indians were killed and nine wounded. These figures are almost certainly low because the Americans found fourteen dead Indians partly concealed under leaves and eleven others on the field of battle. Blood along the trail and blood on two canoes convinced Sullivan's men that a fairly large number of wounded Indians had been carried from the field. The Americans took only two prisoners, one a white Tory and the other a black.

The number of soldiers and Indian warriors who took part in the battle of Newtown is also open to question. Butler was right in speaking of his foe's "superior numbers," but just how many fought on the British-Indian side is not clear. Butler said only six hundred while Sullivan estimated those opposing him at fifteen hundred. The correct figure was probably somewhere in between these two estimates. The Indians may have numbered as many as eight hundred, mostly Senecas, Cayugas, and Mohawks, with about thirty Delawares. Many of their chiefs were present, including Brant. He was the leader of the Indians but had to share his command authority with Cornplanter and Sayenqueraghta of the Senecas. Red Jacket was also on hand and was reported to have been one of the first to flee the battlefield. The British numbered 250 to 300, mostly

Rangers but including a small detachment from the regular army. A number of them were too ill on August 29 to fight. Walter Butler was there, as well as his father, and dropped some private papers and his officer's commission, which were found by the Americans after he retreated.

General Sullivan, writing to the president of the Continental Congress a month after the battle, explained how he arrived at his estimate of fifteen hundred of the enemy, although he said he could never determine the number "with any degree of certainty." He based his figure partly on General Poor's opinion, although he also noted that the two prisoners taken said there were eight hundred opposing him. To arrive at an estimate, Sullivan inspected the field of battle, judging the extent of the breastworks, how far apart the Indians seem to have been placed, and the total area they covered.

John Butler gave his account of the fight in a letter dated September 2 to Lieutenant Colonel Bolton at Niagara. He said he "suspected" at the start what the Americans were trying to do and urged retirement to stronger positions on the hill. Brant and the Cayugas' chief supported Butler but "the Indians were obstinately bent upon staying in the Lines." In the fighting that followed, "both officers & men behaved with much Spirit, but the efforts of such a handful were of little avail.... The Consequences of this affair will, I fear, be of the most serious nature unless there is speedily a large Reinforcement sent in to the country; at any rate those Families whose Villages & Corn have been destroyed will be flocking into Niagara to be supported, and you know the quantity of Provisions that this will consume." In a postscript, Butler added gloomily, "The Rebels are advancing very rapidly...."

That the Americans were much excited by their first real battle with the enemy and very much in a mood to bring as much destruction on them as possible is apparent from the eyewitness accounts they wrote afterwards—although they seldom agree on details. Lieutenant Erkuries Beatty recalled

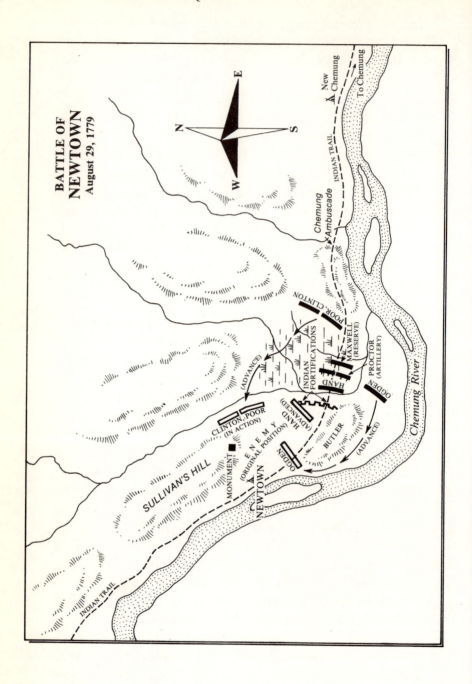

that "the Indians returned the fire very brisk with many shouts for about 2 hours while a disposition was made to attack them." Lieutenant Thomas Blake noted that "as we attempted to ascend and cross the mountain, were fired upon by the Indians, who gave at the same time a most hideous yell which resounded in the mountains as if covered with them." Lieutenant Obadiah Gore thought they must have killed more Indians than they found "as there was great quantities of blood found in their paths." Apparently the army was pleased with its day's work for, he continued, "The troops were much animated with the days success."

As was not uncommon in frontier fighting, the white troops adopted Indian custom and often scalped dead Indians. Lieutenant Beatty, commenting on the difficulty of telling how many of the enemy had been killed, remarked in his journal that "there was 10 or 12 scalps taken which was killed by Genl. Poors brigade on the hill." In the entry in his journal for the day after the battle, Lieutenant Barton reported: "Sent out a small party to look for some of the dead Indians.... Toward noon they found them and skinned two of them from their hips down for boot legs; one pair for the Major the other for myself."

(The Newtown Battlefield Reservation now marks the area of the battle, although if one goes to the picnic grounds one is not on the actual battlefield. On top of the highest hill, just west of where most of the fighting took place, stands the Sullivan Monument, a tall shaft with a tablet on it. Even by car, if one has a knowledgeable guide, the geographical features of the battlefield still can be traced quite easily. In addition to this reservation, the states of New York and Pennsylvania, as well as local authorities and historical societies, have erected over the years tablets and roadside signs that help trace the route of Sullivan's expedition.)

The Battle of Newtown was the only pitched battle of the four-months campaign. At the start more military action had been expected, and even after this victory Sullivan's men anticipated further fighting. The Indians, though, were much disheartened by this show of American power, and neither they nor the British were able to put into the field any force that could match that of Sullivan. The Indians retreated in the face of the American advance for the next two weeks, hastily abandoning their villages and taking to the woods. They harrassed small detachments and caused some casualties but that was all. In a military sense, then, the whole campaign was anticlimactic, casualties were small on both sides, while the Americans were dealing very damaging blows to the Indian economy.

One blow of this kind was struck August 30, the day after the battle, when Sullivans' men destroyed what the general wrote Washington was a "vast quantity of corn" around Newtown. They also burned twenty houses there and thirty about two miles to the east. The soldiers were much impressed with the lush Indian crops. "Our Brigade Destroyed about 150 Acres of the best corn that Ever I saw," wrote Lieutenant Beatty. He said that some of the stalks grew sixteen feet high. They also devastated "great Quantities of Beans, Potatoes, Pumkins, Cucumbers, Squashes & Watermelons, and the Enemy looking at us from the hills but did not fire on us."

The same day General Sullivan had the dead buried and arranged to send the sick and wounded, along with some heavy guns, back down the river to Tioga. He also had some bad news for his victorious troops. The food they were carrying with them would not be enough to see them through the rest of their expedition and return, if they depended entirely on it. Nor were there enough pack horses left to carry supplies. He therefore paraded the troops in the evening and asked them if they would agree to half rations, which meant a half pound of flour a day and a similar amount of beef. The rest of their provisions would have to come from the fruits and vegetables they found growing along the way. These were plentiful in places, but being fresh, and with no way to preserve them, they had on the whole to be eaten on the spot.

Major John Burrowes said the general's proposal "was agreed and answered to by three hearty cheers," while Lieutenant Beatty wrote that it was accepted "with a great deal of chearfullness." A private wrote to a friend that the troops "chearfully submitted" to half rations, "being anxious to extirpate those Hell-Hounds from off the face of the Earth."

The army was now ready to push on toward its uncertain destination.

"The land exceeds any that I have ever seen"

On the last day of August the army was on the march again, through territory of which Major Burrowes wrote, "The land exceeds any that I have ever seen." That day the troops destroyed eight houses at a hamlet two miles beyond Newtown and twenty more at the site of Elmira. At the same time, a detachment of soldiers under Colonel Elias Dayton of the Third New Jersey Regiment was dispatched to the west. These men went eight miles or so in pursuit of some fleeing Indians and wiped out the Indian village at Big Flats, also burning thirty acres of corn and a quantity of hay. A number of feather beds were found in the houses and some chests the Indians had buried in the fields. The main body of the army was marching north and camped that night near the site of the village of Horseheads.

The army set off in a northward direction again on September 1 but spent most of the day struggling through a twelve-mile swamp, "chiefly white and spruce pines," recorded Lieutenant Barton, who also noted that "we forded a creek that runs through the swamp, fifteen different times." Little wonder that Major Burrowes for his part was not surprised at "the men giving out, they having fourteen days provision on their backs exclusive of their other baggage." The swamp and the narrow passages between hills would have been excellent locations for launching attacks by the Indians and Tories but none took place. Presumably this shows how badly demoralized they were by the rout at Newtown.

After a weary day of marching, most of the army reached Catherine's Town, although Clinton's brigade, bringing up the rear, had to spend the night in the swamp. Catherine's Town was a few miles south of the lower end of Seneca Lake, about at the site of the later village of Montour Falls. The Indian village was named for a romantic and already legendary figure, sometimes called Catherine Montour, sometimes Queen Catherine of the Senecas. She was said to be the daughter of Count Frontenac, governor of French Canada, and an Indian woman. Raised in luxury, she was captured when about ten years old by Senecas during one of their expeditions against the French and the Hurons. The Senecas were much taken with her beauty and grace and when she grew up she married a leading chief of the tribe. Catherine began to exert considerable influence in tribal affairs and accompanied her husband to Philadelphia on several occasions when the Six Nations were negotiating with the Americans. Here she was entertained at the highest levels of Philadelphia society.

Other stories about her, though, make her fierce and cruel. According to such accounts she took part in frontier raids and at Wyoming "she followed in the train of the victorious army, ransacking the heaps of the slain, and with her arms covered with gore, barbarously murdering the wounded, who in vain supplicated for their lives." This story seems unlikely to be true. Catherine had fled her town when the Americans arrived and she probably went to Niagara where the British officers would make her welcome. After the war she returned to her home and was supposed to have been paid a visit by Louis Phillippe, the exiled French king. One son was killed in the Revolution.

Catherine's Town was deserted, but fires were still burning

and other evidence indicated it had been abandoned in haste very recently. The village consisted of about thirty houses, which the army destroyed the next day, along with cornfields and fruit trees. The troops also found some livestock, which they took for food. Their most interesting discovery was an aged Indian woman, hiding in the woods, who, Lieutentant Barton thought, must have been a hundred years old. She expected to be killed at once, but instead she was taken to General Sullivan who assured her she would not be harmed. The woman then confirmed that the Indians had left only a few hours before the Americans arrived. She said the women and children had wanted to stay but that the men had made them leave because so many warriors had been killed. She also told of many wounded arriving from the Newtown battle, which, with other evidence found on the march, further convinced Sullivan that Indian casualties had been heavier than first appeared. Sullivan ordered some soldiers to erect a shelter for the squaw and she was given a sizable store of food.

While at Catherine's Town, Sullivan tried to get in touch with the Oneidas, from whom he had expected more help. Using one of the few members of the tribe who was present as a messenger, the general sent word of the victory at Newtown and expressed surprise "that I find only four of your warriors have joined me, though I have far advanced into the enemy's country." Nothing was heard from the courier until he rejoined the army September 19 when it was already on its way home. The scout then had with him only two Oneida warriors and one sachem. Meanwhile, Colonel John Butler was asking for boats to help him transport the British sick, and General Haldimand, from Quebec, was promising to send troops. One message said 860, another only 380. They were to be regular troops, Rangers and Indians, under the command of Sir John Johnson. None of them ever appeared to try to bar Sullivan's advance.

The army was on its way again on September 4, moving north on the eastern side of Seneca Lake after rain in the morning delayed its departure. The following day the village of Kendaia, or Appletown, so named apparently because of extensive orchards, was reached. Here the troops found an elderly man, Luke Swetland, who had been captured at Wyoming the previous year and adopted by a Seneca family. Whether the Senecas had left him behind intentionally or whether he escaped is not clear. He told Sullivan that the Indians had departed three days earlier "in the greatest confusion," and that they had refused John Butler's plea to make a stand at the end of the lake. Swetland also said that Brant had a thousand warriors with him, but this seems unlikely. The twenty houses of Appletown, which Sullivan noted were "neatly built," were, in his words, "reduced to ashes."

After being slightly delayed by cattle and horses that strayed and had to be rounded up, the American force on September 7 reached Kanadesaga (Geneva) at the northern end of Seneca Lake. Also known as Seneca Castle, it was an important town, on a main route, and Brant and Butler stopped here after the Cherry Valley massacre to divide spoils and prisoners. Sullivan expected the Indians to make a stand at this place if anywhere. Accordingly, he approached it with care and with the hope of surrounding any enemy force in it. Brigades were sent to the right and left while the rest of the army approached from the center, but the settlement of fifty or so houses was deserted. Here also were the ruins of a stockade that Sir William Johnson had built in 1756 to encourage the Indians to assist the British.

The only living person the Americans found was a white male child about three years old. One account, written a hundred years later when the centennial of Sullivan's campaign was being observed in upstate New York, asserted:

> This child was evidently of Dutch parentage, and had probably been captured on the Pennsylvania border. It could speak a few Indian words. When

found it was entirely naked and nearly starved. General Sullivan took a great interest in the little waif, and caused it to be placed in a panier or basket on a pack-horse, in which conveyance it accompanied the army until its return to Wyoming. Captain Machin of the engineer corps had the little fellow christened Thomas Machin, and its nourishment was derived from an excellent cow which shared all the vicissitudes of the campaign and returned in safety to Wyoming. The child was taken to New Windsor, near Newburgh, at the end of the campaign, where it soon died of small-pox. No clue to its identity was ever discovered.

The army remained at Kanadesaga through September 8, first of all destroying the houses and the crops. The men found Indian "trinkets," which they appropriated. Sullivan sent a detachment of four hundred men along the west side of the lake to destroy a village known as Gothseunquean and another unit marched east toward Cayuga Lake to put the torch to Scawyace. While this work of destruction was going on, Sullivan prepared to send another group of incapacitated men back to Tioga with fifty soldiers to guard them. Unknown to the general, Washington the day before had reported to Congress that the expedition was already a success. Colonel Bolton, at Fort Niagara, on the other hand was pessimistic in writing to General Haldimand in Quebec, saying he had little hope of effective aid from the Indians against the Rebels. Only the Senecas and Mohawks could be counted on. In a report dated September 10 he feared for the safety of Niagara itself. The Americans, he wrote, "by all accounts are determined to pay us a visit" but he would defend the fort "to the last extremity."

At Geneva the expedition surveyed the situation to see whether the provisions on hand would allow an advance even as far as the Genesee River, let alone Niagara. Major Burrowes confided to his journal on September 8: "Living already hard. We eat meat twice in three days, & bread once in four or five days. The country abounds with corn and beans which we solely live on. Salt very scarce." The decision was to continue marching, and on September 9 the army marched out, this time headed to the west toward Canandaigua. In Iroquois the word means "town-set-off," that is, a place selected for settlement. On the way the troops had once more to struggle through "a very thick and deep swamp that continued the remainder of the days" before they "entered into an open country, that was free from timber."

The army marched on another fourteen miles on September 11 to Honeoye, at the northern end of the lake of that name. Honeoye in Iroquois means "finger-lying," and the traditional story is that it derives from an incident in which an Indian, bitten by a snake, cut off his finger to keep the poison from entering his body further. There were only ten houses here to destroy and Sullivan decided to build a small fort where everything not needed for the final dash to the Genesee could be stored. A detachment of fifty men under Captain Cummings was left in charge.

Of the final goal, which Sullivan called "Chinesee," he repeated what prisoners told him, that it was

> the grand capital of the Indian country; that Indians of all nations had been planting there this spring; that all the rangers and some British had been employed in assisting them, in order to raise sufficient supplies to support them while destroying our frontiers; and that they themselves had worked three weeks for the Indians when planting. This information determined me at all events to reach that settlement, though the state of my provisions, much reduced by unavoidable accidents, almost forbad the attempt. My flour had been much reduced by the failure of the pack-horses, and in the

passage of creeks and defiles; and twenty-seven of the cattle had been unavoidably lost. We, however, marched on for the Chinesee town.

Continuing west, the army passed the northern end of Hemlock Lake, then turned south between it and Conesus Lake, the farthest west of the Finger Lakes. Near its southern end, on September 13, they reached the village of Conesus, with twenty-five houses and the usual "large quantity" of vegetable crops. Conesus was the home of Chief Big Tree, described as "a former friend of the Americans." The army stopped four hours to destroy the homes and crops and began to build a bridge over a creek that could not be forded.

Before proceeding further toward the Genesee, Sullivan needed more information as to the location of the "Genesee Castle" that was reputed to be the largest Seneca town. The general expected to find it on the east side of the river, near where Canaseraga Creek enters the Genesee. He did not know that the older town of Chenussio, about at this spot, had been abandoned and that the place he wanted, best known now as Little Beard's Town for the Seneca chief, was on the west side of the river. Indian villages were usually moved every few years to secure new crop land and because it was easier to move to a new supply of bark and building wood for houses than to bring them to the old village. Sullivan rather angrily denounced his maps later as "erroneous and calculated to perplex rather than to enlighten." Nor did Sullivan have any competent guides, at least among his white troops. Probably not a soldier in the army had ever seen the Genesee.

To determine what route he should take and to avoid falling into a trap, Sullivan decided to send out a small scouting party, and he thereby touched off the unfortunate and bloody events that came to be known as the Groveland Ambuscade. Groveland was the later name of a township west of the lower end of Conesus Lake and east of the river. He chose Lieutenant Thomas Boyd of Morgan's Riflemen to lead a party of three or four soldiers and two Oneidas, a chief and Lieutenant Hanyost Thaosagwat. For reasons unknown, Boyd took it upon himself to enlist a larger party that totaled twenty-six when he set out.

Boyd was a native Pennsylvanian and was twenty-two years old at this time. He and his two brothers all served in the Revolution and followed their mother's admonition "never to disgrace their swords by any act of cowardice." Thomas's brother William was killed at Brandywine. Lieutenant Boyd was described as "a very sociable and agreeable young man, strongly built, and brave even to rashness." Sullivan may have known of Boyd's reputation, for he cautioned him of the dangers of the mission. All he wanted him to do was to explore the route to the Genesee as unobtrusively as possible and to try to find out how many Indian enemies lay along the route. There was reason to believe the number was considerable. Boyd was to set out on the night of September 12, and Sullivan hoped he would be back early the next morning.

Boyd made a mistake in taking so large a party. It was too small to be able to fight any considerable force of the foe, but too big to be able to reconnoiter without making its presence known. Nor did anyone on the American side know that John Butler and several Indian leaders, including Brant, Cornplanter, and Little Beard, were plotting an ambush of the American army when it next moved. A large force, perhaps as many as five or six hundred Indians and Rangers, set up the ambush where the army, after crossing the bridge being built, would have to enter a swamp. A further mistake occurred when Boyd's party had to choose between two paths. The one they should have taken led northwest, directly to Little Beard's Town, but they followed a path that ran nearly due west.

The route they took led Boyd and his men to the village of Gathtsegwarohare, about seven miles from their starting point. They found it abandoned but with fires still burning. When daylight came on the thirteenth they prepared to enter

"The land exceeds any that I have ever seen" 77

the village, and as they did so two Indians appeared from one of the houses. A scout, Timothy Murphy, who boasted of already having taken thirty-two scalps, could not resist firing his rifle at one of them. The Indian fell dead, Murphy scalped him and also took his moccasins. The other Indian escaped to give warning, and the rifle shot may have been heard by the enemy, thus destroying the chance of keeping the scouting party's presence secret.

Boyd sent four of his men back to report to Sullivan what they had found so far. Two of the men apparently returned to Boyd with news of Indians in the vicinity while the other two continued on toward the army's camp. Meanwhile the main part of the group also began to make its way back to the army. On the way they saw from time to time a warrior start up and run away from them. Boyd wanted to give chase but the Oneida scout warned him the Indians were merely trying to lead them into a trap. Boyd's men got within two miles of safety when they stumbled on the ambush the Indians and British had prepared for the army. The Indians far outnumbered Boyd's party and only a few escaped, including Murphy, although one account says that a dozen made it back to camp. Boyd, Sergeant Michael Parker, and Thaosagwat were captured. His elder brother was in the Indian force and accused Thaosagwat of treachery. He, however, would not harm his own brother, but the Senecas might do as they pleased with him, whereupon Little Beard killed him with his sword. The Indians scalped and mutilated the dead soldiers and Thaosagwat, hacking the latter's body to pieces.

When Sullivan heard the survivors' tale he ordered Hand's brigade to the relief of Boyd, not knowing that it was already too late. The rescue force found that Boyd's misfortune had saved the army from a possible disaster as the ambushers had all fled, leaving behind equipment and provisions. Hand's men came upon the bodies of six of Boyd's men and buried them in a common grave. In the meantime Butler (there are conflicting stories as to whether this was Colonel John Butler or his much hated son Walter), after questioning Boyd and Parker, sent them under a Ranger guard to Little Beard's Town. What happened next is also disputed. By one account Colonel Butler intended to send the two to Fort Niagara as prisoners of war, but the Indians overpowered the Rangers and seized the captives. Another account insists Walter Butler was happy to hand them over to the Senecas to be tortured.

Sullivan moved the army forward, over much the same route Boyd had taken, and spent the night of September 13 at Gathtsegwarohare, which was destroyed. Marching northward on the fourteenth, still looking for Genesee Castle, the general discovered that it was across the river. The troops crossed the Genesee about a mile north of what is now Mount Morris. Judging by comments in journals, the officers and men found the Genesee River and its valley a beautiful sight amidst the bloodshed and uncertainty of war. The river rises in the Allegheny Mountains in northern Pennsylvania and flows north for about 158 miles, emptying into Lake Ontario just north of Rochester. One journal entry called the valley "a large fruitful plain," while another made note of grass so tall it hid the men marching through it.

The day before, when most of Boyd's party failed to return from its brush with the foe, one officer wrote "it is to be feared [they] have fell a sacrifice to their [the Indians'] barbarity." These words turned out to be only too true, as the army learned when it reached Little Beard's Town, which consisted of 128 houses, the largest found on the expedition. In Iroquois, Little Beard's Town was De-o-nun-da-ga-a and was located about where Cuylerville now stands. It lay 280 miles from Easton and was the farthest west the expedition was to get. Sullivan said the houses were "mostly very large and elegant." Tories as well as Senecas had lived here, and it was, indeed, the headquarters of the tribe. "The town was beautifully situated," Sullivan continued, "almost encircled with a clear flat which extends for a number of miles, where the most extensive fields of corn were, and every kind of vegetable that can be conceived."

The normal rural beauty of the scene was forgotten when Sullivan's men discovered the fate of Boyd and Parker. The general summed it up later:

> It appeared they had whipped them in the most cruel manner, pulled out Mr. Boid's nails, cut off his nose, plucked out one of his eyes, cut out his tongue, stabbed him with spears in sundry places, and inflicted other tortures which decency will not permit me to mention; lastly, cut off his head, and left his body on the ground with that of his unfortunate companion, who appeared to have experienced nearly the same savage barbarity.

Lieutenant Gore wrote simply that they were "butchered in the most savage and inhuman manner possible." Boyd and Parker were buried with military honors and Lieutenant Robert Parker paid tribute to Boyd in his journal: "Inspired with every Heroe's virtue he fell a victim to their savage barbarity in defence of the injured rights of mankind."

The Americans also found at Little Beard's Town Mary Jemison (1743–1833), known as "The White Woman of the Genesee." She was born at sea while her parents were en route to America from Ireland. In 1758, during the French and Indian War and while living in western Pennsylvania, she was captured by a war party and taken to Fort Dusquene. There she was given to two Seneca women and adopted into the tribe. She was married twice, the first time to a Delaware and the second time to a Seneca, becoming the mother of eight children in all. She said of her second husband that "he uniformly treated me with tenderness, and never offered an insult." Jemison also told how he took two white prisoners in a battle and burnt them alive in "a fire of his own kindling." When she had a chance to go back to the white world she refused and became a well-known figure in the life of the Senecas in western New York. Walter Butler and Brant often visited her home.

Jemison had moved to Little Beard's Town in 1762 and

apparently did not flee when the Americans approached. She told Sullivan's horrified men another detail of the torture of Lieutenant Boyd that has since been questioned but not disproved. According to her, Boyd's abdomen had been cut open and his intestines pulled out and wound around a tree while he was still alive. Jemison was given a tract of land on the Genesee, near Castile, in 1797, and in 1817 the state of New York officially confirmed her title to it.

(In 1841 the remains of Boyd and Parker and of the others who died earlier in the ambush were removed to Mount Hope Cemetery in Rochester and reburied there on "Revolutionary Hill." In 1927, preparatory to observing the 150th anniversary of the expedition in 1929, the Livingston County Historical Society acquired the plot of land between Geneseo and Cuylerville where Boyd and Parker had originally been buried, including the traditional "Torture Tree," which was still standing. The site became the Boyd-Parker Memorial Park.)

At Little Beard's Town, or Genesee Castle, the army also found another white woman who had been taken prisoner at Wyoming in 1778. She told of Butler's gathering the force of Indians to try to ambush Sullivan and of the subsequent flight from the town toward Niagara, which they expected would be attacked as soon as Sullivan could march there. She also said the Indian women had begged the warriors to sue for peace. The woman's husband had been killed by the Indians and she had with her a small son, who, however, died on the way home.

As usual, the town was completely destroyed and all the crops, too. Colonel Dearborn and Lieutenant Beatty both recorded in their journals that the army began this task at six in the morning and did not finish until two in the afternoon. Most of the corn was burned along with the houses, but some was got rid of by throwing it in the river. Estimates of the number of bushels of corn destroyed ranged from fifteen thousand to twenty thousand. Lieutenant Barton, who also helped ravage the town, wrote as the time to depart came, "This place very rich and good."

General Sullivan decided not to press the expedition further but to start for home. He was informed that there were no more Seneca villages to the west, and he did not think it wise to try to capture well-defended Fort Niagara, about seventy-six miles away, with his supplies running low. The men had already been on half rations for more than two weeks. Even if he pushed on successfully, it was getting too late in the season to go farther west and still get back to Wyoming before cold weather set in. If the expedition had not been delayed so long past its original starting time he might have felt able and obliged to pursue the enemy further. If he started back now he could attack the country of the Cayugas, the next of the Six Nations to the east, on the way. In the language of the time and sounding the way generals do, he addressed this message to his troops:

> The commander-in-chief informs this brave and resolute army that the immediate objects of this expedition are accomplished, viz.: total ruin of the Indian settlements, and the destruction of their crops, which were designed for the support of those inhuman barbarians, while they were desolating the American frontiers. He is by no means insensible of the obligations he is under to those brave officers and soldiers whose virtue and fortitude have enabled him to complete the important design of the expedition, and he assures them he will not fail to inform America at large how much they stand indebted to them. The army will this day commence its march for Tioga.

The message was issued on September 15, and the army began retracing its steps that day, destroying any overlooked cornfields. Near Conesus the men found fourteen bodies of

Boyd's party, which were buried. Colonel Bolton at Niagara, meanwhile, was still worrying about being attacked and reported Indians and their families arriving for protection. At Honeoye on September 17 the army found the supplies they had left there safe, guarded, as Lieutenant Barton recorded, by "a captain and fifty men, exclusive sick, lame and lazy."

Arrived at Canandaigua on September 18, Sullivan found an Oneida chief and three of his tribe who told him that one hundred Oneidas and Tuscaroras had started out to join the expedition but for some reason or other had returned home. The Oneidas asked Sullivan not to punish the Cayugas, but two days later, at Geneva, Sullivan's council of war decided against peace with them. Accordingly, Lieutenant Colonel William Butler, commander of the Fourth Pennsylvania Regiment in Hand's brigade, was dispatched with six hundred men to go south along the east shore of Cayuga Lake and destroy all the villages he could find. By September 28, when he rejoined the rest of the army, Butler had destroyed Cayuga Castle and four other towns with about one hundred houses and two hundred acres of corn.

On the same day Butler set out, September 20, Sullivan sent Colonel Peter Gansevoort eastward toward the Mohawk River. Gansevoort was well known for the gallant stand he made as commander at Fort Stanwix in 1777 when it was besieged by the British and Indians under St. Leger. He was ordered to destroy the lower Mohawk Castle at Fort Hunter and to go on to Albany, which he proceeded to do, burning one village of twenty houses on the way. At the lower Mohawk Castle Gansevoort found only four houses occupied, the rest of the Mohawks having fled. He would have destroyed the place as ordered, but a number of Patriot frontiersmen, who had themselves had their homes burned down by the enemy, prevailed on him to let them move in. Another side excursion that began on September 20 was that of Colonel William Smith who, with two hundred men, was dispatched southward along the west side of Seneca Lake to destroy Kershong and any other settlements he found.

The west side of Cayuga Lake was as yet unattended to, and so on the twenty-first Colonel Dearborn and two hundred men started south in that area. They laid waste six Cayuga villages with their farmlands and orchards. They also captured four Indians, one male and three females. The day before Dearborn set out, Major Jeremiah Fogg, perhaps reflecting a new feeling among the troops, wrote, "We now suppose ourselves at home and quite out of danger from the savages." But army life went on much as before: "This morning [the twenty-second] there was great appearance of a storm. Marched sixteen miles. A sore mortality among old horses, twenty died this day besides about sixty were shot by the rear guard."

From Niagara John Butler wrote that he had had to retreat to Niagara because of lack of supplies and that he suspected General Sullivan was moving to attack Fort Oswego. He claimed the Iroquois remained "unshaken in their attachment to His Majesty's cause." Two days later, however, Colonel Bolton correctly reported that Sullivan was on the way back to Tioga.

The army reached Catherine's Town on September 23, and one of the first sights to greet them was the old Indian woman they had left when they passed through on the way north. She was, reported Major Fogg, "Just as we left her, twenty days before in her bark hut, with a quart of corn by her." The men also found the body of another Indian woman who had been dead for three or four days. They were forced to conclude that she probably had been wantonly shot by one or more American messengers on their way through the area.

Continuing south on September 24, the army paused to kill forty or fifty of its pack-horses. One account says they were killed because they were too weak to go on while another says they were killed for food for the men. Perhaps both are right. According to the popular tradition, the heads of the horses were lined up along the trail, either by Indians or by some of the soldiers, and this is the source of the name of the later village of Horseheads on this site.

Pressing on through Bear Swamp on the same day, the army reached Camp Reid (or Reed), so-called for a Captain Reid who had led a detachment up from Tioga to meet the returning troops. The camp was located in what is now the southeastern corner of the city of Elmira. Reid brought with him various supplies, including one hundred head of cattle and "a plenty of flour, spirits, &c." The food was a most welcome change after the vegetable diet the men had been on. The army rested here five days, having a barbecue of five oxen one day with a ration of liquor for everyone. Having previously heard that Spain had also entered the war on the American side, Hand's brigade lighted thirteen fires and drank thirteen toasts to celebrate.

The expedition continued to seek out and destroy any settlements it missed on the way north, but for the most part the remainder of the march was devoted to getting home. Tioga was reached on September 30, where another celebration took place, including a war dance directed by an Oneida chief in which General Hand took part so that even a "grave chaplain could not repress a smile." Wyoming was reached on October 7 and Easton on October 15. Two days later a thanksgiving service was held and soon thereafter most of the army was on its way to New Jersey to join General Washington's forces.

In his report to Congress, Sullivan estimated that in all 160,000 bushels of corn, as well as other fruit and vegetables, had been destroyed. He said forty Indian settlements had been put to the torch and that, except for one village, "there is not a single town left in the country." This is probably an exaggeration, although Guy Johnson the next month wrote that "almost all the villages" were gone. As to casualties, "this army has not suffered the loss of forty men, in action or otherwise." Sullivan then praised his troops: "I feel myself much indebted to the officers of every rank for their unparelleled exertions, and to the soldiers for the unshaken firmness with which they endured the toils and difficulties attending the expedition."

Safely back in Easton, officers and men had matters of their own to attend to and think about. Lieutenant Colonel Hubley, concluding his journal, called the expedition a "glorious achievement" that "will make no inconsiderable balance" in American affairs. "Ages hence," he thought, the nation will celebrate "those brave Sons, who nobly resigned their lives." But he also had a note of criticism for the "unparallel'd and unpardonable neglect" in the supply situation.

Lieutenant Beatty found that the clothes he had left with "the Wash woman" had been stolen while he was away. Nevertheless, he "went out in the Country" and had "Buckwheat Cakes, Butter, Milk & honey which was a very great rarity indeed." Later he "drank some excellent wine" and "so I believe I may here end my Journal with a belly full of good wine."

"... the very graves of their fathers"

"I flatter myself," General Sullivan stated near the end of his report to the Continental Congress on his expedition, "that the orders with which I was entrusted are fully executed." Congress officially agreed, thanking him for "effectually executing" the campaign against the Indians who, "encouraged by the councils and conducted by the officers of his Britannic majesty, had perfidiously waged an unprovoked and cruel war against these United States, laid waste many of their defenseless towns, and with savage barbarity slaughtered the inhabitants thereof."

Nevertheless, there was criticism. Sullivan had captured neither Fort Niagara nor Oswego, which in the beginning it was hoped he would do. Given all the objectives set by Washington and the distances to be traveled, it seems unlikely he could ever have attacked both. Perhaps, if he had not waited so long for supplies at Wyoming, he could have gone on to Niagara and attempted its capture. This leads to the further question as to whether Sullivan was justified in insisting on so much in the way of material before he set out. No general ever has enough men, enough guns, enough supplies of every kind to satisfy him. Sullivan's problem was compounded by the difficulty in those days, without prepared foods, canned goods, decent roads, or large self-propelled vehicles, of taking enough provisions with him even if he had them. The men, as noted, lived off the land a good deal of the time, but had to subsist mostly on vegetables, and there is considerable evidence that the steady diet of corn was hard on the soldiers' digestion. Quite likely the expedition had done as much as the human beings who made it up were capable of doing under the circumstances.

The most important question to be asked was: Had the expedition ended once and for all the danger of further attacks by the Iroquois? Summing up his accomplishments, Sullivan in his report claimed "nor is there even the appearance of an Indian on this side of Niagara." In a sense, the general was right. The Indians had fled before him, all the way from Newtown to the Genesee. But they had been all around him during this time, even though they dared not attack. The expedition had killed very few of them, and as soon as the army withdrew, the Indians were free to return to their homes if they could solve the problem of food. As Major Fogg wrote in bringing his journal to an end, "The nests are destroyed, but the birds are still on the wing."

In short, the Indians were defeated but not conquered. If Niagara had been taken they might have given up on their British allies and sued for peace with the Americans. As it was, they flocked to that post to ask for food, clothing, and shelter, so that by the beginning of fall five thousand of them were around the fort. In other words, the Iroquois were more dependent on the British than ever and so would gain nothing by abandoning them. The Senecas especially would never forget the summer of 1779. The warriors for once were outmatched and unable to fight back effectively. In addition, their whole way of life had been disrupted. But being Indians—and human beings—what had been done to them made them furious at the Americans and burning to get revenge.

The Iroquois, however, were in for more suffering before they could hope for vengeance. The winter of 1779–80 was an especially severe one in New York State. The western part of the state was under five feet of snow most of the winter. Deer and other animals died, and the Indians could not find the game they needed for food to help keep them alive. Hundreds of them must have died of freezing and starvation. This natural disaster may well have made them even more bitter about the troubles inflicted on them by the Sullivan expedition.

As early as February 1780, when the ground was still heavily covered with snow, Indian war parties began forming and going out in different directions to resume the war against the American settlers, now more hated than ever. On March 21, for example, the garrison at Skenesboro, consisting of thirteen militiamen, was surprised and captured. Brant, leading a party of Indians and whites, came upon a group of men making maple sugar on April 7. Three were killed and the other eleven taken prisoner. Sir John Johnson came down from Canada in May with five hundred Indians and whites and in the neighborhood of Johnstown laid waste a dozen miles of countryside north of the Mohawk River. At least nine persons were killed and thirty-three captured.

The pro-British Iroquois, chiefly the Senecas and the Mohawks, also put pressure on the Oneidas and Tuscaroras, who had been friendly to the Rebels. Under threats of superior force many of them were induced to move to the Niagara area where they would be under the eyes of the British. Brant burned Oneida and Tuscarora settlements, killing any cattle he and his party could not take with them. About four hundred of the Oneidas and Tuscaroras fled to Fort Stanwix to seek the protection of their American friends.

The Canajoharie district was raided in August by four hundred Indians and Tories, including Cornplanter and Brant. As was not uncommon, some Indian women were along to secure any plunder they might come upon. Fifty-three houses were burned, as well as barns and other structures. The raids went on, culminating in October in the devastation of the Schoharie Valley, around the area where Schoharie Creek flows into the Mohawk about five miles west of Amsterdam.

Sir John Johnson led this raid, which included Canadian troops and British regulars, as well as Rangers and about 265 Indians. The raids of 1780 were for the most part in regions not reached by General Sullivan, but these were the areas where the Indians had to attack if they were to strike back. Almost all the territory covered by Sullivan's expedition was as yet devoid of white settlements.

By the fall of 1780, 330 Americans had been killed or captured, over seven hundred houses and barns burned, six forts and several mills destroyed, and seven hundred head of cattle seized. A great amount of grain was also destroyed. In an area not yet heavily settled, this was a disaster and left the region in much the same condition the Seneca lands had been reduced to the year before. As one future president, James Madison, wrote to another, Thomas Jefferson, as early as June 2, 1780, "The expedition of General Sullivan against the Six Nations seems by its effects rather to have exasperated than to have terrified or disabled them." Nor was the bloodshed ended. In 1781 the Indians were back on the warpath, and nearly three thousand of them, in more than sixty parties, ranged the frontier areas of New York, Pennsylvania, and the Ohio region.

Through this period, in comments on events, the words "barbarity" and "barbarous" crop up regularly—as in Congress's vote of thanks to General Sullivan. It is easy to tell from the journals kept by officers and men on the expedition that they took for granted that the Indians were "savage barbarians." Sullivan's officers drank a toast: "Civilization or death to all American savages." From that point of view, the Indian methods of warfare—scalping and torture, for example—were barbarous, but they were accepted as normal by the Indians, friend and foe alike. So far as cruelty to persons or wanton killing of civilians, the expedition's record was good, even if not perfect. The Indians and their British supporters claimed, of course, that burning homes and destroying crops was barbarous. Or is it an acceptable way of winning a war once one gets involved in fighting? Nearly a century later, General William Tecumseh Sherman led a Union army through Georgia and other Southern states, laying waste as much of the farms and their produce as he could. This certainly seemed barbarous to those, mostly noncombatants, who suffered as a result, especially when the acts were committed by their fellow citizens. Yet Sherman's march may have shortened the war and thus could have reduced deaths and suffering. General Sherman said, "War is hell."

Judge Thomas Jones of Long Island, a leading and vocal Loyalist, put the matter this way:

> Though the Americans complained heavily of the burning and plundering of Fairfield and Norwalk, in the State of Connecticut . . . as an act of inhumanity in the British . . . yet in their annual Thanksgiving . . . their ministers did not forget to return thanks to Almighty God for the success which had attended Sullivan's burning, plundering, cruel, marauding, distressing expedition against these Indians, the allies of Britain. So that, what the New England rebels termed barbarity in the British was deemed a righteous, godly and Christian-like act when perpetrated by themselves.

In relation to other events of the American Revolution, both before and after, the Sullivan expedition had little noticeable effect. It was the main American effort of 1779, but it made no particular mark on the state of affairs between the British and the Patriots. In the northern colonies, its progress was followed with keen interest and apparently much talked about. Newspapers printed long accounts in the form of letters from participants, who told of events that had taken place quite some time before the story got into print. The European settlers had been fighting Indians in frontier skirmishes almost since the day they first landed and founded their towns, but never before had a full-scale army been dispatched to wage war as though on another white nation.

The expedition, in fact, involved one of the largest and most complex military campaigns of the entire Revolution. Nevertheless, it did not cause British forces of any consequence to be diverted from other activities. At this point in the war, Britain was more concerned with the part being played by France and Spain, especially the former. There was also growing opposition to the war in England, while in the colonies neither the Americans nor the British seemed able to come to grips in such a way as to settle the conflict once and for all. The final British surrender at Yorktown came almost two years to the day after Sullivan's troops marched back into Easton. In a sense, the Americans could lay claim to having conquered the territory of the Six Nations, but they withdrew entirely, not even leaving small garrisons. The Patriots' right to permanent possession might well be debated, especially after the events of 1780, which weakened the American hold on the interior of New York State.

When the war did end and the Americans won independence, the Iroquois found themselves abandoned by their British allies. In concluding peace between the two countries, no provision was made for the Six Nations. The British ceded the thirteen colonies and all the land west to the Mississippi to the United States and so, in effect, turned over to the new nation all the Indians that inhabited that vast and fertile territory. Most of the Iroquois had been faithful to their treaties with the British but now stood to lose more than any other group by the results of the Revolution. The Iroquois had always prided themselves on abiding by treaties, whether with white men or other Indian tribes. No wonder they were now angry at the British. It is only fair to say that the British officers and officials resident in North America who carried the burden of direct dealings with the Iroquois were greatly embarrassed by these events. For a long time they had urged the Indians to help the British as the best way of retaining their ancestral lands. Now there was nothing they could do or say to placate or console their recent allies.

For all their treaty making with the Indians and their better than average treatment of them, the British had never thought of the Iroquois as being sovereign in the same sense the British were. They granted the Indians the right of occupancy but looked upon themselves as the national state that exercised sovereign power over New York along with the other colonies. The Indian concept was that no one "owned" the land in that sense. The League of the Iroquois was concerned with relations among themselves and with other Indian tribes, not with governing the land they occupied, the land that gave them the necessities of life.

The Revolution's end meant that the Iroquois not only lost their land but also that, for practical purposes, the league was crushed and could function no more. The Revolution had split the Iroquois, just as it had divided the white settlers, and so the unity that had been the bedrock of their strength was gone. They had also suffered heavy losses in warriors and in possessions as a result of the frontier fighting and Sullivan's expedition. Facing an uncertain future with the Americans, they must have been fearful of what these bitter enemies would do to them.

In a longer historical view, though, it was not the Revolution that caused the fall of the League of the Iroquois. The seeds of the collapse were planted as soon as the first Europeans came to the New World, to take land from the Indians and, worst of all, to embroil the Indians in their own quarrels. The Iroquois were first caught up in the struggle between the British and the French, then in the war between the British and the Patriots. When the white men came, the Iroquois were building an empire, consolidating their power over other Indians in a large part of the northeast, and developing the league into a practical form of government. Perhaps, if Europe had not intruded on them for another century or two, the Iroquois might have developed their civilization further. The arts of peace would have had at least a chance of appearing, and the Iroquois might have become the Romans of North America. As soon, though, as the white men came, much of Indian life revolved around the relationship between the races, rather than among the Indians themselves. A civilization that is advanced technologically always changes a less advanced society in its image, rather than the other way around.

After two centuries the Iroquois were for the first time completely at the mercy of the white men. The Treaty of Paris of 1784 ended the Revolution and made formal the authority of the United States over the Indian lands. The new nation must now formulate an Indian policy and deal on a government-to-tribe basis with the Iroquois and others. Many Americans wanted to drive the Indians out of New York State entirely, but George Washington and Philip Schuyler, among others, opposed this. They wanted to treat the tribes in a more humane manner. Before any negotiations took place between the victors and the Indians, however, the former had to settle an internal problem: Did the individual states or Congress control the land the Indians occupied? This would determine which party had the right to negotiate. A great deal was at stake. The Continental Congress on behalf of the thirteen colonies had accumulated a large debt, and the currency was unstable. If the Indian territory were national public land, Congress could sell acreage to meet its financial problems and it could grant land to veterans to make up for pay they had been promised but had never received. The states wanted to stake their claim to these lands for much the same reasons. On top of that, some of the states, such as New York and Massachusetts, each claimed the same land in certain western areas because the royal charters that had made the original colonial grants were vague as to geographical locations and boundaries.

New York took steps in the spring of 1784 to make a treaty with the Iroquois. Governor Clinton invited the Mohawks,

Onondagas, Cayugas, and Senecas to a council at Fort Stanwix and deputies from these tribes and the state commissioners gathered there on August 31. The commissioners then sent messengers to the Oneidas and Tuscaroras who arrived in a few days, explaining they had not come earlier because they had not been invited. The state delegation thought Samuel Kirkland, the missionary, was to blame for their attitude because he was urging them to resist any attempt by the state to secure any of their land. Later, though, Kirkland became active in helping some land developers purchase large acreages from the Indians.

The council formally got under way on September 5, with Brant and Cornplanter among the important Indian delegates. One of the advisers to the state commissioners was Peter Gansevoort, now a general, while another future president, James Monroe, was on hand to observe on behalf of Congress. Everyone expressed generous sentiments, Governor Clinton calling for a settling of differences, establishing boundaries and promoting trade. Brant on the part of the Iroquois approved of bringing about peace and friendship but said his delegation had no authority to negotiate about land. The council adjourned on September 10, with everyone expressing good will but without any land being ceded by the Indians, which was an objective high on the list of New York goals.

Congress very shortly sent commissioners to hold its own council meeting with the Iroquois in October. The commissioners were Oliver Wolcott (1726–97), Arthur Lee (1740–92) and Richard Butler, the first two having already played moderately prominent roles in the Revolution. Wolcott was from Connecticut, was a signer of the Declaration of Independence, and since 1775 had been an Indian commissioner, trying at that time to secure Iroquois neutrality. Lee was a member of the active and influential Lee family of Virginia who had carried out several missions abroad attempting to secure foreign aid for the colonies during their struggle for independence. This meeting was also to be at Fort Stanwix, and Brant was there before the meeting started. He, however, was called to Niagara by family affairs. There was at this time a great deal of illness among the Indians, which Brant described as a "Bilious Fever."

An impressive participant in the meeting was the Marquis de Lafayette, the French nobleman who had come to the United States and served energetically in the cause of the Patriots. The Indians listened to Wolcott, after which Cornplanter replied for them in a friendly manner. Then Lafayette spoke, criticizing the Iroquois for having fought the French earlier. An Indian replied, saying frankly that the Iroquois had always sided with the English because the French "always begun unjust Disputes." Years later, Red Jacket claimed he was the one who made this speech, but it is not even certain that he was at Stanwix at the time.

In the end, the American commissioners got from the Iroquois by treaty more than Sullivan's army had been able to secure by force of arms. In another sense, the Indians had to give up by conquest what they had originally secured by the same means. The Treaty of Fort Stanwix was signed on October 22. By its terms, the Iroquois ceded some land around forts, a four-mile strip from Niagara to Buffalo Creek and all claims to lands of the Ohio region and westward. They also were required to give six hostages to guarantee the safe return of all prisoners held by them. The Oneidas and Tuscaroras, who had sided with the Americans, were assured they could keep the land they lived on. In return the commissioners, "in execution of the humane and liberal views of the United States ... will order goods to be delivered to the said Six Nations for their use and comfort."

New York State kept nibbling away at the land of the Iroquois. In June 1785, the government prevailed upon the Oneidas to cede half a million acres, and so those who had been allied to the Americans were the first to be squeezed off their land. Gradually, more and more land was obtained by treaty or by fraud until the people of the once mighty Six

Nations were herded onto reservations or forced to move west. The British, meanwhile, were making a practical gesture to take care of their allies. A large tract in southern Ontario was given to the Mohawks, and by 1785 more than eighteen hundred Indians, including members of other tribes, were settled there. Others moved elsewhere, most of the remaining Oneidas, for example, migrating to Wisconsin in the 1820s. In the end some of the fading remnants of the Six Nations moved west of the Mississippi River.

While the old world of the Iroquois was collapsing, two of the main figures responsible for bringing them to their post-Revolution situation were continuing their careers along different lines. General Sullivan's military career was over. His many complaints over the years, including those made while his expedition was being organized, led Congress to appoint a committee to investigate his charges. While the committee was at work, Sullivan offered his resignation, giving ill health as the excuse. In November the resignation was accepted on a permanent basis, not temporarily, as Sullivan had expected. It was not a glorious end to a military career that, whatever its ups and downs and however much Sullivan had only himself to blame, was honorable. More unlucky than incompetent, Sullivan had been a loyal soldier, devoted to the Patriots' cause.

Back home in New Hampshire, he was welcomed officially and with enthusiasm. He agreed to return to Congress in 1780, but first he resumed his law practice and set about restoring his personal finances, which had suffered by his long absence in the army. In Congress, Sullivan was involved in a number of arguments, such as those concerning the conflicting claims of New Hampshire and New York to Vermont. His congressional career ended in August 1781, and he returned home after having served seven years in Congress and the army. He was now forty-one years old. He was not, however, through with public service, for he was a delegate to the convention that wrote a new constitution for New Hampshire in 1782. In 1785 he ran for the office of president (governor) of the state but came in a poor third in the voting. The following year, though, he was successful and in 1787 was reelected. When a large number of citizens, who wanted more paper money issued in order to make it easier for debtors to meet their obligations, threatened to use force, Sullivan called out the militia, put down the uprising, and seized forty prisoners.

The new Constitution of the United States was offered for approval in 1787, and Sullivan worked hard to secure New Hampshire's ratification of it, but this was not achieved until June 1788. In the meantime he had been defeated for president in 1788, then elected once more in 1789. In October of that year Washington, now first president of the United States, appointed Sullivan a federal judge. Washington that same month visited New Hampshire and Sullivan had a reunion with his former commanding general for the first and only time since he left the army.

The last years of Sullivan's life were unhappy ones. He fell badly in debt, took to drinking excessively, and deteriorated into senility, probably as a result of a nervous disease as well as the drinking. He was unable to perform his judicial functions after May 1792. Sullivan died on January 23, 1795, in his fifty-fifth year. The story told of the odd events at his funeral are probably true. The law at the time allowed creditors to attach the body of a deceased debtor and hold it from burial until the debts were paid. Such an attempt was made at Sullivan's rites, whereupon his friends sent for his former army comrade, Joseph Cilley. Now a general, Cilley had been a colonel commanding the First New Hampshire regiment during the expedition against the Iroquois. Eleven miles away at the time of the funeral, Cilley dashed to the scene on horseback, drew two pistols, and threatened to kill anyone who interfered. He then walked with the coffin, pistols in hand, until it was safely put into the ground.

To the Iroquois, George Washington was Ha-no-da-ga-nears, which means "Town Destroyer," and this remained the name they gave to all presidents of the United States. When Cornplanter addressed Washington in 1790, pleading with the United States to keep its promise to leave the Indians in possession of their land, he said, "Our women look behind them and turn pale, and our children cling close to the necks of their mothers" when your name is heard. Nevertheless, because of what he believed were Washington's just dealings with the Iroquois, the religious leader Handsome Lake said years later that the general was the only white man allowed to enter the heaven of the Indians. (Edmund Wilson says that the name Town Destroyer was first applied to George Washington's grandfather, John, and that George inherited the name, even before the Revolution and Sullivan's expedition, which is usually given as the occasion for the coining of the term.)

After the Revolution, many officers and men who had served under Washington, Sullivan, and other generals, but whose names are not found in the history books, were in a mood to move west and become pioneers. They were encouraged in many cases by grants from the states. New York, for example, offered six hundred acres to each enlisted man and more to officers, setting aside 1,500,000 acres of Indian land in the Finger Lakes region as a military tract for this purpose. Some ex-soldiers sold their rights to the land, but many moved in. The participants in Sullivan's expedition were much impressed with the lovely, fertile region they saw on their long march, and some of them came back after the war to carve out farms, but they were only part of a strong, steady movement westward that began once the Revolution was won and the Indian menace ended.

The *Historical and Statistical Gazetteer of New York State* for the year 1860 recounts many instances of early settlers in the upstate areas who were veterans of the Revolution. The first settler in one Delaware County hamlet was a Squire Whittaker who was a survivor of the Wyoming Valley raid. The *Gazetteer* notes that among the early settlers in Schuyler

County, in which was located Catherine's Town, were "many of the soldiers" who had marched through it with Sullivan. At Seneca Falls in Seneca County the first permanent settler, ten years after Sullivan's expedition, was Lawrence Van Clief, who had been on that march and who also had spent the hard winter at Valley Forge.

The most enthusiastic account and one that seems to express in flowery language the general sentiment of men of the time as to the future of the region was penned by Lieutenant Robert Parker. Let us, he wrote,

> suffer our imaginations to Run at large through these delightful wilds, & figure to ourselves the opening prospects of future greatness which we may reasonably suppose is not far distant, & that we may yet behold with a pleasing admiration those deserts that have so long been the habitation of beasts of prey & a safe asylum for our savage enemies, converted into fruitful fields, covered with all the richest productions of agriculture, amply rewarding the industrious husbandman by a golden harvest; the spacious plains abounding with flocks & herds to supply his necessary wants.
>
> These Lakes & Rivers that have for ages past rolled in sacred silence along their wonted course, unknown to Christian nations, produce spacious cities & guilded spires, rising on their banks, affording a safe retreat for the virtuous few that disdains to live in affluence at the expense of their liberties.

This journal entry is an almost perfect expression of the belief that America was the promised land, a new Garden of Eden, where Americans would produce a better race by seeking a living, as well as virture and independence, each on his own plot of land. It took for granted, too, that these virtuous Americans had a right to drive out the "savage enemies." Parker saw the end of the war one way; the editor of the *Gazetteer*, however, saw it from the Indian viewpoint:

> At the conclusion of the peace, the force and spirit of the Indians were annihilated, and they quietly yielded to the gradual encroachment of the whites, until the last acre of their hunting grounds . . . and the very graves of their fathers, passed out of their possession.

A Reading List

Alden, John Richard. *The American Revolution: 1775–1783*. New York: Harper & Row, 1954.

Beauchamp, William M. *A History of the New York Iroquois*. Albany, N.Y.: New York State Education Department, 1905.

Colden, Cadwallader. *The History of the Five Nations, Depending on the Province of New-York in America*. Ithaca, N.Y.: Cornell University Press, 1958.

Cook, Frederick, ed. *Journals of the Military Expedition of Maj. Gen. John Sullivan, Against the Six Nations of Indians in 1779*. Auburn, N.Y.: Knapp, Peck & Thomson, 1887.

Ellis, David M., Frost, James A., Syrett, Harold C., and Carman, Harry J. *A Short History of New York State*. Ithaca, N.Y.: Cornell University Press, 1957.

Flick, A. C., ed. *The Sullivan-Clinton Campaign in 1779: Chronology and Selected Documents*. Albany, N.Y.: The University of the State of New York, 1929.

Graymont, Barbara. *The Iroquois in the American Revolution*. Syracuse, N.Y.: Syracuse University Press, 1972.

Hunt, George T. *The Wars of the Iroquois: A Study in Intertribal Trade Relations*. Madison, Wis.: University of Wisconsin Press, 1940.

Lancaster, Bruce, and Plumb, J. H. *The American Heritage Book of the Revolution*. New York: American Heritage, 1958.

Morgan, Lewis Henry. *League of the Iroquois*. Secaucus, N.J.: The Citadel Press, 1962.

Norton, A. Tiffany. *History of Sullivan's Campaign Against the Iroquois*. Lima, N.Y.: A Tiffany Norton, 1879.

Stone, William L. *The Life of Joseph Brant.* New York: Alexander V. Black, 1838.

Swiggett, Howard. *War Out of Niagara: Walter Butler and the Tory Rangers.* New York: Columbia University Press, 1933.

Wallace, Anthony F. C. *The Death and Rebirth of the Seneca.* New York: Alfred A. Knopf, 1970.

Whittemore, Charles P. *A General of the Revolution: John Sullivan of New Hampshire.* New York: Columbia University Press, 1961.

Wilson, Edmund. *Apologies to the Iroquois.* New York: Farrar, Straus & Giroux, 1960.

Wright, A. H., comp. *The Sullivan Expedition of 1779: Contemporary Newspaper Comment & Letters.* Ithaca, N.Y.: A. H. Wright, 1943.

Writers' Program of the Work Projects Administration in the State of New York, comp. *New York: A Guide to the Empire State.* New York: Oxford University Press, 1940.

Index

agriculture, 28
Albany, 6, 7, 9, 10, 25, 36, 49, 82
Alden, Colonel Ichabod, 15-16
Algonquin Indians, 23
Allegheny River, 13, 46, 47
American Indians, 1-2, 4-11, 13, 14-17, 18, 19-37, 90, 91, 94, 97, 99, 101
American Revolution, 2, 4, 5, 6-8, 9, 11, 17, 19, 22, 26, 35, 40, 47, 70, 76, 91-93, 94-95, 99
Amsterdam, 4, 89
Anglican Church, 11
Anne, Queen, 26
Appletown. *see* Kendaia
Arnold, General Benedict, 9
artillery, 49, 53, 56, 58-61
Augusta, 17

Barton, Lieutenant William, 61, 65, 69, 71, 80, 82
Battle of Brandywine, 44, 49, 76
Battle of Germantown, 44, 49, 50
Battle of Long Island, 6, 43, 49, 50
Battle of Newton, 60-65, 71
Battle of Oriskany, 8, 11, 37, 49
Battle of Princeton, 44, 49, 50
Battle of Trenton, 43-44, 49, 50
Bear Swamp, 84
Beatty, Lieutenant Erkuries, 63, 65, 66, 67, 80, 85

Big Flats, 69
Big Tree, Chief, 75
Binghamton, 9
Blake, Lieutenant Thomas, 65
Bolton, Lieutenant Colonel, 63, 73, 82, 83
Boston, 42, 46, 48, 50
Boston Tea Party, 5
Boyd, Lieutenant Thomas, 75-80, 82
Boyd-Parker Memorial Park, 80
Braddock, General Edward, 49
Brant, John, 26
Brant, Joseph, 10-11, 12, 15, 16, 22, 26, 37, 62, 63, 72, 76, 79, 89-90, 95-96
Brantford, 11
British, the, 1-2, 6-10, 13, 15, 25, 26, 35, 36-37, 40-41, 42-46, 49, 50, 57, 60-62, 66, 70-72, 74, 77, 82, 88, 90, 91-93, 96, 97
Brodhead, Colonel Daniel, 47-48
Buffalo Creek, 26, 96
Bunker Hill, 42, 50
Burgoyne, General John, 6-7, 41, 47
Burrowes, Major John, 67, 69, 73-74
Butler, John, 10, 13, 14, 57, 59, 62, 63, 71, 72, 76-78, 83
Butler, Richard, 95
Butler, Walter, 10, 15-16, 50, 63, 77-78, 79, 80

108 *Index*

Butler, Colonel William, 82
Butler, Colonel Zebulon, 14, 53
Butler's Rangers. *see* Tory Rangers

Campbell, Thomas, 15
Camp Reid, 84
Canada, 2, 6, 9, 11, 23-24, 25, 36, 39, 42-43, 47, 49, 50, 70, 89, 90
Canajoharie, 47, 89
Canandaigua, 74, 82
Canaseraga Creek, 75
Castile, 80
Catawba tribe, 24
Catherine, Queen. *see* Montour, Catherine
Catherine's Town, 70, 71, 83, 100
Cayuga Castle, 82
Cayuga Lake, 73, 82, 83
Cayuga tribe, 19, 21, 22, 36, 62, 63, 81, 82-83, 95
Champlain, Samuel de, 25
Chemung, 56, 59
Chemung Ambush, 56
Chemung River, 55, 59-60
Chenussio, 75
Cherokee tribe, 24
Cherry Valley, 13, 15-17, 72
Chinesee. *see* Little Beard's Town
Cilley, Colonel Joseph, 49-50, 98
clans, 27, 31
Clinton, Brigadier General James, 46-47, 48, 51, 56, 57-59, 61, 70
Clinton, General Sir Henry, 7-8, 47
Clinton, George, 47, 94-95
clothing, Indian, 27-28
Cobleskill, 9
Colden, Cadwallader, 34

Conesus, 75, 81
Conesus, Lake, 75
Connecticut, 10, 11, 14, 37, 91, 95
Constitution of the United States, 98
Continental Army, 1, 6, 9, 11, 39-41, 42, 50, 59
Continental Congress, 35, 36, 39, 42, 43, 45, 51, 63, 77, 84, 87, 90, 94, 95, 97
Cooper, James Fenimore, 35, 46
Cooperstown, 57
Cornplanter, 13, 15, 36-37, 62, 76, 89, 95, 96, 99
Cornwallis, General Charles, 10
Crown Point, 25
Cummings, Captain John, 55, 74
Cuylerville, 78, 80

dances, Iroquois, 29-30
Dayton, Colonel Elias, 49-50, 69
Dearborn, Colonel Henry, 49-50, 61, 80, 83
Declaration of Independence, 52, 95
Deganawidah, 20-21
Delaware County, 99
Delaware River, 9
Delaware tribe, 24, 47, 62, 79
d'Estaing, Comte, 46
Detroit, 39, 50
Dunlap, Reverend Samuel, 16
Dutch, the, 23, 25

Easton, 1, 46, 48, 50, 52, 78, 84, 85, 92
Elmira, 59, 69, 84
Erie tribe, 24

False Face societies, 31
Fellows, Sergeant Moses, 59
festivals, Iroquois, 30-31

Finger Lakes, 75, 99
Five Nations. *see* Six Nations
Fogg, Major Jeremiah, 83, 88
Fort Clinton, 47
Fort Dearborn, 50
Fort Duquesne. *see* Fort Pitt
Fort Edward, 7
Fort Hunter, 82
Fort Niagara, 1, 4, 5, 10, 36, 40, 59, 63, 70, 73, 78, 80, 81, 83, 87-88, 89, 96
Fort Orange. *see* Albany
Fort Pitt, 46, 47-48, 49, 79
Fort Stanwix, 8-9, 10, 49, 82, 89, 95, 96
Fort Sullivan, 59
Fort William and Mary, 42
Forty Fort, 13-14
France, 2, 17, 92
French, the, 4, 17, 23, 25, 40, 46, 70, 93, 96
French and Indian War, 2, 4, 5, 8, 10, 11, 14, 26, 40, 41, 47, 49, 50, 79
Freud, Sigmund, 31
Frontenac, Count, 70
fur trade, 23, 24-25, 31

games, Iroquois, 29
Gansevoort, Colonel Peter, 8-9, 82, 95
Gates, Major General Horatio, 7, 41, 43
Gathtsegwarohare, 76-77, 78
Genesee Castle, 75, 78, 80
Genesee River and Valley, 19, 24, 26, 34, 46, 48, 73, 74-76, 78, 79, 80, 88
Geneseo, 80
Geneva. *see* Kanadesaga
George III, King, 36, 87
Georgia, 91
German Flats, 9

Gore, Lieutenant Obadiah, 65, 79
Gothseunquean, 73
Grant, Sergeant Major George, 55
Great Britain, 2, 4, 17, 92
Greene, Major General Nathanael, 43, 44
Groveland, 75
Groveland Ambuscade, 75-80

Haldimand, General, 71, 73
Hand, Brigadier General Edward, 48-49, 52, 53, 56, 58-61, 77, 82, 84
Handsome Lake, 13-14, 36, 99
Hemlock Lake, 75
Herkimer, Brigadier General Nicholas, 8
Herkimer, 9
Hiawatha, 20-21
Honeoye, 74, 82
Horseheads, 69, 83-84
Howe, General Sir William, 6, 7, 8, 43
Hubley, Lieutenant Colonel Adam, 52, 85
Hudson River and Valley, 2, 6, 8, 17, 26, 47
hunting, Iroquois, 28
Huron tribe, 23-25, 70

Illinois tribe, 24
Iroquois Indians, 1-2, 4-11, 13, 15, 18, 19-37, 39, 41, 46, 53, 55-56, 69-80, 82-84, 87-89, 92-96, 98-99, 101

Jay, John, 51
Jefferson, Thomas, 50, 90
Jemison, Mary, 79-80
Jesuits, the, 24-25
Johnson, Guy, 5-6, 11, 84

Index

Johnson, Sir John, 5-6, 36, 71, 89-90
Johnson, Sir William, 4-6, 10, 11, 72
Johnstown, 89
Jones, John Paul, 18
Jones, Judge Thomas, 91

Kanadesaga, 72-73, 82
Kendaia, 72
Kershong, 83
Kingston, 8, 47
Kirkland, Samuel, 37, 51, 52, 95

Lackawanuck, 53
Lafayette, Marquis de, 96
Lake Champlain, 6
Lake Erie, 19, 24, 26
Lake Ontario, 1, 26, 34, 78
Lake Superior, 21, 24
language, Iroquois, 33-34
League of the Iroquois, 19-23, 31, 93
Lee, Arthur, 95
Lewiston, 26
Little Abraham, 36
Little Beard, 15-16, 76-77
Little Beard's Town, 74-76, 78-80
Livingston County Historical Society, 80
London, 11
Longfellow, Henry Wadsworth, 20
longhouses, 26-27
Loyalists, 1, 2, 6, 8-9, 10, 16, 17, 37, 40, 47, 62, 70, 89, 91

McCrea, Jane, 7
Machin, Captain, 73
Machin, Thomas, 73
Madison, James, 90
Massachusetts, 1, 49, 58, 94

matriarchy, Iroquois, 27
Maxwell, Brigadier General William, 48-49, 53, 58-60
Michigan, 24
Minisink, 9
Mississippi River, 23, 24, 92, 97
Mohawk Castle, 82
Mohawk River and Valley, 2, 4, 6, 8, 9, 10, 26, 47, 50, 82, 89
Mohawk tribe, 10, 11, 15, 19, 20, 21, 22, 23, 24, 25, 26, 27, 32, 33, 36, 62, 73, 89, 94-95, 97
Monmouth, 17
Monroe, James, 95
Montour, Catherine, 70
Montour Falls, 70
Montreal, 6
Morgan, Lewis Henry, 34-35
Morristown, 18
Mount Morris, 78
Murphy, Timothy, 77

Neutral Nation, 24
New England, 2, 7, 17, 91
New Hampshire, 1, 41, 42, 50, 58, 61, 97-98
New Jersey, 17, 18, 43-44, 45, 50, 58, 60, 69, 84
Newport, 17, 45-46
Newtown, 59-60, 66, 69, 88
Newtown Battlefield Reservation, 65
New York City, 2, 6, 8, 34, 40, 50
New York State, 1-2, 4, 6, 7, 9, 13, 19, 23, 25, 34, 35, 39-40, 48, 58, 60, 65, 80, 88, 90, 92, 94-95, 96, 97, 99
Niagara River, 1, 24, 26, 34
North Carolina, 20, 23

Ogden, Colonel Matthias, 60
Ohio, 90, 96
Ohio River, 4

Oneida tribe, 7, 10, 19, 21, 22, 33, 37, 58, 71, 76, 77, 82, 84, 89, 95, 96-97
Onondago tribe, 19, 20, 21, 22, 36, 95
Ontario, 23, 25, 97
Oswego, 26, 37, 40, 83, 87
Otsego Lake, 46, 47, 57

Parker, Lieutenant Robert, 52, 79, 100-101
Parker, Sergeant Michael, 77-80
Patriots, 2, 5, 6-10, 11, 14, 16, 17, 36-37, 39-40, 42-43, 44, 82, 89, 91, 92, 93, 96, 97
Pennsylvania, 1, 4, 8, 39-40, 44, 46, 47-48, 58, 65, 72, 76, 78, 79, 90
Philadelphia, 7, 17, 34, 36, 43, 49, 70
Phillippe, Louis, 70
Poor, Brigadier General Enoch, 49, 53, 58-59, 61-63, 65
Proctor, Colonel Thomas, 49, 53, 56, 58
Pulaski, Casimir, 17

Queen Esther's Castle, 55

Rebels. *see* Patriots
Red Jacket, 13-14, 36-37, 62, 96
religion, Iroquois, 30-31
Rhode Island, 45-46
Rochester, 78, 80
Romney, George, 11

sachems, 21-22
St. Lawrence River, 19
St. Leger, General Barry, 8-9, 10, 82
Salamanca, 48
Saratoga, 7, 17, 41, 49, 50
Savannah, 17

Sayenqueraghta, 62
Scawyace, 73
Schenectady, 47
Schoharie Valley, 6, 89
Schuyler, General Philip, 41, 94
Schuyler County, 99-100
Seneca Castle, 72
Seneca Falls, 100
Seneca Lake, 71-72, 82
Seneca tribe, 13, 14, 15, 19, 21, 22, 23, 24, 26, 27, 34, 35, 36, 41, 47, 62, 70, 72, 73, 75, 77-78, 79, 81, 88, 89, 90, 95
Sherman, General William Tecumseh, 91
Six Nations, 19-23, 26, 33, 36, 37, 40-41, 57, 70, 81, 90, 92, 96-97
Skenesboro, 89
Smith, Colonel William, 82
South Carolina, 23, 24
Spain, 84, 92
Staten Island, 45
Stony Point, 18
Sullivan, Major General John, 1-3, 9, 17, 18, 37, 40-46, 48, 49, 51-53, 55-63, 65-66, 71-72, 73-78, 80-81, 84-85, 87-88, 90, 97-98, 99
Sullivan expedition, 1-2, 11, 39-41, 50-85, 87-88, 90-93, 96, 99-100
Sunbury, 52
Susquehannah tribe, 24
Susquehanna River, 1, 9, 13, 45, 52, 53, 55, 57
Swetland, Luke, 72

Tennessee, 23, 24
Thaosagwat, Lieutenant Hanyost, 76-77
Thayendanegea. *see* Brant, Joseph, 10

Index

Thomas, Brigadier General John, 42
Tioga, 46, 53, 55, 56-58, 66, 73, 81, 83, 84
Tories. *see* Loyalists
torture, 32-33, 79-80
Tory Rangers, 8, 10, 13, 14, 15, 60, 62-63, 71, 76, 78, 90
Treaty of Fort Stanwix, 4, 96
Treaty of Paris, 94
Tuscarora tribe, 7, 20, 22, 37, 82, 89, 95, 96

Unadilla, 9
United States, 40

Valley Forge, 45, 50, 100
Van Clief, Lawrence, 100
Vermont, 97

wampum, 22
war chiefs, Iroquois, 21-22
warfare, Indian, 31-32

War of 1812, 50
Washington, General George, 2, 6, 15, 17, 18, 36, 39-41, 42-44, 45, 46, 48, 51-52, 57, 62, 66, 73, 84, 87, 94, 98, 99
Washington, John, 99
Wayne, Brigadier General Anthony, 18
weapons, Iroquois, 29, 32
Westchester, 6
West Point, 17-18
Whittaker, Squire, 99
Willett, Colonel Marinus, 49-50
Wilson, Edmund, 35, 99
Wisconsin, 97
Wolcott, Oliver, 95-96
Wyalusing, 53-54
Wyoming, 1, 9, 13, 14-15, 48, 50-51, 53, 55, 57, 59, 70, 72, 73, 80, 81, 84, 87
Wyoming Valley, 13-15, 52, 99

Yorktown, 10, 47, 92